Praise for
The World of Creativity

"So fascinating, I couldn't stop reading. Amazing format: he pulls you to a different corner of the world every few pages for a unique local encounter to inspire a new view. Travelogue and creative insights combined make me daydream double-time. Absolutely adorable even for short attention spans."
— Derek Sivers, TED speaker on How to start a movement (+26 million views) and author of *How to Live*.

Fredrik Haren has given us more than a book about creativity—he has created a bridge connecting human wisdom from every corner of our world. Essential reading for anyone who believes creativity can make us more human."
— Dorji Dhradhul, Creativity Catalyst, Former Director General, Royal Government of Bhutan (Tourism Council)

"Understanding creativity isn't just about generating ideas - it's about unlocking the potential in people. When we nurture creativity, we spark innovation, build stronger, more connected teams, and forge deeper partnerships with our customers and communities. Fredrik Haren is helping crack the code on achieving a global mindset by showing how creativity transcends borders and brings us closer to one another."
— Ling Hai, President for Asia Pacific, Europe, Middle East & Africa, Mastercard

"Fredrik is an ambassador for creativity. His wide-ranging book is a source of encouragement to all who seek to live their lives in a creative spirit'."

—John Adair, author of *The Art of Creative Thinking*

The World of Creativity is a fascinating book that explores creativity through a global lens, featuring insights from diverse professionals and cultures. Fredrick emphasizes that creativity is inspired and often contradictory, advocating for an open-minded approach rather than a rigid framework. The book also highlights various "creative moments", alongside introducing unique concepts such as "unalienizing" (making new ideas familiar) and "creative fractaling" (understanding sub-processes). Ultimately, the text positions creativity as a journey of self-discovery and continuous learning, encouraging readers to embrace curiosity, resilience, and a balance of confidence and humility.

—Andrew Grant and Dr Gaia Grant PhD.
Authors of *Who Killed Creativity?* and *The Innovation Race*
Directors of Tirian Innovative Solutions

"What a thrilling ride - not just around the world, but deep into ourselves. So buckle up, as Fredrik Haren takes you on a journey to explore where true creativity comes from, through the eyes of others and through honest reflection within. This book will make you think and reflect, and I love books that do that! Inspiring, eye-opening, and deeply human."

—Yaron Flint, Author of *Innovative Business Development*

Fredrik Haren insists that we're all far more creative than we realise – and in this book, he unfolds that truth through an inspiring journey around the world, showing how creativity already lives within people as different as a potter in Thailand, a nomad in Mongolia, and a designer in Denmark. Fredrik shares techniques to help us tap into that same universal creative force – one that can transform how we solve problems, spark new ideas, and uncover hidden opportunities. This isn't just about becoming more creative – it's about awakening the creativity that's already within us.

— Mette Refshauge, VP Corporate Communication & Sustainability, A.P. Moller Maersk

"Over the past twenty years, I've worked with some of the world's leading thought leaders, and Fredrik Haren's brilliance truly stands out. His insights into creativity are exceptional, driven by a relentless curiosity and a global journey to uncover human ingenuity in all its forms. What sets Fredrik apart— and earns him the title The Creativity Explorer—is his ability to distil wisdom from every corner of the world and share it with clarity and heart. The World of Creativity is more than a book—it's an inspiring call to action, urging each of us to unlock our own creative potential in a world that needs it now more than ever."

— Andrew Vine, Founder, The Insight Bureau

"In an age where algorithms outpace intuition and automation threatens the soul of originality, "The World of Creativity" is a powerful reminder of what makes us irreducibly human. Creativity isn't a luxury; it's a lifeline. With stories from across the globe, it invites readers into a living tapestry of imagination, courage, and inspired action. One line in particular stands out: "Creativity is inspired." Yes, because it cannot be manufactured, predicted, or optimized by code alone. In a world increasingly engineered for efficiency, this book is a defiant, joyful manifesto for wonder. If your goal is to stay human while shaping the future, start here."

— Dr Mark van Rijmenam, Author,
Futurist and Founder of Futurwise

"As someone who champions the power of the creative industries to unleash human potential, I know that creativity is our most valuable economic asset. Fredrik Haren's extraordinary journey across 37 countries proves this isn't just theory—it's reality. From tech hubs to traditional crafts, from corporate boardrooms to artist studios, this book reveals how creativity drives everything we do. A must-read for anyone who wants to harness the creative force that's reshaping our world."

— Caroline Norbury, Chief Executive Officer, Creative UK

"Fredrik's book is a rare gem. It doesn't just talk about creativity—it embodies it. This book is a global, soul-searching journey that strips creativity down to its raw, human essence. And that's exactly why it matters for implementation.
Implementation thrives on insight, not just instruction. If you want to lead change, build new business models, or deliver bold strategies, you need to be creative—not in theory, but in real, situational, adaptive ways. Fredrik shows us how creativity lives around the world.

This book pushes you to be curious and challenge your assumptions.
— Robin Speculand, Author of Implement: Doing it Right in a Digital World and World's Best Bank - A Strategic Guide to Digital Transformation

"Fredrik doesn't just breathe creativity. He lives it. His endless curiosity is what makes him The Creativity Explorer. In his book, he invites us to become one.
This isn't a book that teaches creativity. It awakens it.
You won't walk away with a formula. You'll leave with something more powerful: a deeper understanding of how you create.
Welcome to The World of Creativity, where every page is an invitation to explore."
— Tay Guan Hin, APAC Regional Director, The One Club for Creativity.

"Haren's book provides us with a delightful atlas that maps out the basics of the creative process. Filled with practical insights from down-to-earth people the world over, it's a fun and informative read!"
— Roger von Oech,, Author of, A Whack on the Side of the Head: How You Can Be More Creative

"If you care about building something that matters, read this. If you care about building something that lasts, read it again."
— Ben Rennie, Author, Lessons in Creativity

"Fredrik Haren has created something extraordinary—a global masterclass in human creativity that will transform how you think, work, and innovate. Drawing insights from 37 countries and thousands of creative minds, this book proves that the best ideas come from the most unexpected places. Essential reading for leaders who know that our biggest challenges require our most creative responses."

— Tom Kindermans, Managing Director,
SAP Central & Eastern Europe

"Fredrik Haren is the Anthony Bourdain of creativity—a fearless explorer who ventures into the most unexpected corners of our world to discover the universal truths about human imagination. Like Bourdain with food, Haren reveals that the most profound creative insights come not just from elite institutions, but from nomads in Mongolia, glass artists in Spain, and children in Mumbai slums. Deeply human storytelling about what makes us create."

— Dr Jerome Joseph, CSP, GSF, HoF,
Author of The Brand Playbook

"Breakthroughs in medicine stem from innovation often driven by the creative minds of scientists and researchers collaborating with one another and new technologies. Fredrik Haren's global exploration uncovers the universal principles of human creativity. This inspiring book reveals how unlocking our creative potential can help leaders drive the innovations needed to change the life of people in a positive way."

— Mark Sonne Kharazmi, VP Executive Office, Novo Nordisk

THE WORLD OF CREATIVITY

BY **FREDRIK HAREN**, THE CREATIVITY EXPLORER

THE WORLD OF CREATIVITY

A JOURNEY ACROSS 37 COUNTRIES TO DISCOVER
THE SECRETS OF CREATIVE MINDS

CAPSTONE
A Wiley Brand

Registered office
John Wiley & Sons, Inc., 111 River Street, Hoboken, NJ 07030, USA
John Wiley & Sons Ltd, The Atrium, Southern Gate, Chichester, West Sussex, PO19 8SQ, United Kingdom

Editorial Office

John Wiley & Sons Ltd, The Atrium, Southern Gate, Chichester, West Sussex, PO19 8SQ, United Kingdom

For details of our global editorial offices, customer services, and more information about Wiley products visit us at www.wiley.com.

Wiley also publishes its books in a variety of electronic formats and by print-on-demand. Some content that appears in standard print versions of this book may not be available in other formats.

Library of Congress Cataloging-in-Publication Data

ISBN 9781907312892 (paperback)
ISBN 9781907312908 (epub)
ISBN 9781907312915 (ePDF)

Cover Design: André Wognum
Author Photo: © Amar Ramesh
Printed and bound by CPI Group (UK) Ltd, Croydon, CR0 4YY

C9781907312892_131125

The manufacturer's authorized representative according to the EU General Product Safety Regulation is Wiley-VCH GmbH, Boschstr. 12, 69469 Weinheim, Germany, e-mail: Product_Safety@wiley.com.

Dedicated to Elaine – With each passing day, I'm more certain that marrying you was the best idea of my life.

And to Lucas, Maria and Sophia: I am in awe watching you grow up to be such wonderful human beings. You are the best of me and the best of your mother – but most of all, you are so wonderfully you! I am so happy you are my children. You make my life complete.

Be a creativity explorer

Welcome to The World of Creativity.

In this book, we are going to go on a journey together to explore the creative process; with the aim of discovering our full creative potential.

To 'explore' means to 'venture into unknown territory in order to learn something about it'. It's about going into uncharted territory to broaden one's understanding of the world. To be curious enough to go beyond our current worldview.

To be a Creativity Explorer is about being interested in broadening one's understanding of the creative process. It is about understanding that creativity can be so much more than we thought it was.

---

*Each page of this book contains one bolded sentence—the author's key point.

How to get the most out of this book

To get the most out of reading this book, I am going to encourage you to do three things; the same three things I used while researching and writing this book:

(1) Be curious
(2) Be open-minded
(3) Be positive

Read with the intention of really wanting to learn something new, something that will help you understand creativity better.

Be a Creativity Explorer.

Fredrik Haren

P.S. If you have feedback on this book, know of someone I should interview about creativity or just want to send some thoughts that came out of reading this book, please drop me an email at **fredrik@fredrikharen.com**. I would love to hear from you.

---

*Please note: QR codes for all links mentioned throughout this book can be found at the back for easy access.

Introduction

You cannot master that which you do not understand.

If you want to master being creative, you have to understand how creativity works. This book is, in no way, meant to be a comprehensive work that covers all the aspects of the creative process – that would be a very thick book, if it were even possible to write. But this book is meant to present you with many different aspects of the creative process.

For many of these aspects, you will be introduced to new terms and descriptions in order to make it easier to grasp the idea discussed. When Mihaly Csikszentmihalyi wrote his famous book *Flow*, he popularised the word 'flow' to describe 'the mental state of a person completely immersed in an activity'. Flow had, of course, always existed, but without a word to describe the concept, it was hard to discuss it, develop it or even be aware of it. **Words help us think. In the same way, I will introduce new words and terms to describe other aspects of the creative process that need a description.** Terms like 'bispective', 'manfred' and 'the videmus moment'. Do not worry if you initially become overwhelmed by all the new terms introduced in this book, and do not be afraid if your first reaction to a new word is to discard it. That is a normal reaction; flow sounded weird, too, when it was first introduced. But with a curious and open mindset, these new terms will help you broaden your understanding of the creative process.

While the goal of this book is to help you become more creative, it's not a 'traditional' creativity book filled with exercises or techniques. While I am not against creativity exercises, I believe that actual creative development does not come through doing creativity exercises, and genuinely creative people seldom use traditional creativity exercises as part of their process. Instead, they are obsessed with understanding their own creative process while, at the same time, being humbled by how little we actually understand about how creativity really works.

So, can creativity be taught at all? Yes. Everyone can learn to become more creative. But creativity is, more than anything, inspired, not taught through standard exercises or methods.

Inspiration

My father, a musician and a music teacher, was often asked by his students' parents, 'How does a child become a musician?' He would reply that you can teach any child to play an instrument. Just show them how to hold their hands, read the notes and handle the instrument, and they will be able to play it after a while. But the only way to turn someone into a musician is through inspiration. Expose them to the musical greats, play the classics and the all-time hits. Introduce them to the musical geniuses. And if they are ready to absorb this inspiration, they become musicians.

I think this is true, not just for musicians, but for all kinds of creative expression. I also think it is true for creativity itself.

Creativity is inspired.

And while I am going to ask you to reflect on the different messages presented in each chapter, and while I hope you will gain new insights into the creative process from the examples shared in this book; my overarching ambition with putting this book together is that the sheer number of different examples, the diversity of people you will meet, the variety of cultural and professional backgrounds that are presented as well as the parade of human stories that you will be served will breathe inspiration into you.

In short, I hope to inspire your creativity.

Each chapter in this book is centred around one insight about creativity that I learnt from meeting with creative people while travelling around the world for the last 25 years. My exploration of creativity has taken me to more than 75 countries across 6 continents, and I have visited most of these countries multiple times. My quest to understand human creativity has taken me to between 15 and 35 countries *per year*, and on each of these trips I have met with at least one creative person – often, of course, many more than one. During this quarter-of-a-century-long journey, I have, in total, met with thousands of creative people from all walks of life.

Together we will now journey around the globe and learn from creative professionals around the world, like a choreographer in Copenhagen, a Swedish master chef, a Spanish glass artist and many more. The kind of people you would expect to learn from in a book with the title *The World of Creativity*.

But we will also learn from more unexpected professionals. People with jobs that are not normally considered 'creative', like a Maldivian hotel manager, a pastor from Berlin and a government official in Bhutan. Because creativity is everywhere. The diversity of professions, industries, cultures and countries featured is deliberate. It's there to invite you to look for creativity all around you.

Finally, we will also be going to a few places that usually would never be considered to be featured in a creativity book; like the Mongolian desert and the slum of Mumbai. We will even venture to North Korea. I am aware that I have visited those places from a position of privilege; financial, socioeconomic, and passport privilege, to mention a few. But for me, it was important to explore *all* kinds of places. To feature only successful creative professionals from my own Western cultural bubble would have been safe and easy. But it would also have been wrong. Privilege is tricky, but ignorance is worse.

I also understand that I risk offending or provoking some readers by sharing something positive that came out of a visit to a dictatorship like North Korea. Or that the power dynamics between a global keynote speaker visiting teenage girls in a Mumbai slum could be seen as troubling. I often contemplated excluding some chapters from this book, but doing so would have been wrong. **If we want to understand human creativity – and that is my passion in life – we have to be open and willing to look everywhere, and to learn from everyone**. Not going, I think, would have been a worse use of privilege. Not listening to these girls, for example, would be worse than listening to them. (I have decided that 10% of the royalties this book generates will be donated to Kranti (https://www.kranti-india.org) – the organisation empowering the girls from India's red-light areas to become agents of social change and happiness. I encourage you to also donate some money to them.)

If there is anything my extensive travel and my deliberate decision to venture far from my bubble of familiarity have taught me, it would be that listening to and learning from people who live very different lives than yours is the most meaningful thing you can do because it gives you perspective. Perspective not only on your life, but on life itself. In this book, I will share the positive insights around creativity that these encounters brought me, because that is the scope of this book.

Let me also add a caveat: If I were to write a book about food and include, say, a chapter about what I learnt about sushi while visiting Japan, that would not suggest that I think everyone in Japan only eats sushi. It would only mean that my trip to Japan inspired me to write about how learning about sushi expanded my knowledge about food. In the same way, this book is about the insights into creativity that inspired me on my journeys. The chapters should not be read as sweeping generalising descriptions of the people of the countries I visit, but as insights gained from being a visitor there. For example, Americans eat sushi and people in Japan eat hamburgers, and there are, of course, gentle creative people in other countries than Vietnam and not all Vietnamese people are gentle creatives. But, my visit to Saigon to meet with gentle, creative Vietnamese creatives got me reflecting on the power of gentle creativity.

With the lessons and insights from all these encounters with creative people from all over this beautiful blue dot floating through space, we can start to build a picture of what creativity means for ourselves.

Every chapter ends with a reflection to encourage you to take the insights from the people featured in each chapter and turn them into your own insights about your very own creative process – and/or to inspire you to act on them.

The beautiful contradiction that is creativity

This book is not written in the format of traditional creativity books, which often tend to introduce one overarching framework meant to describe 'the truth' about how creativity works.

The truth is that there is no *single truth* about how 'creativity works'. There is no one framework that can describe the creative process because there are as many creative processes as there are people.

Some people have their best ideas when brainstorming with others, while others have their best ideas when they are alone.

Some people thrive on pressure and deadlines to generate their best ideas. Others find that deadlines kill their creativity.

Some creatives will wait for inspiration while others believe inspiration comes when you start to create.

And so on.

Often, one person will use different, sometimes opposite, creativity approaches on different occasions.

Study enough creative people and you will come to the conclusion that if one is to write about the creative process, one has to accept the beautiful contradiction that is creativity.

That is why this book, at first glance, might sometimes seem to contradict itself. How one chapter is about acting on ideas when they come, while another chapter is about profound patience. Or how one chapter is about individual creativity and another about collective creativity, and so on. This is done on purpose. If you want to be comfortable with creativity, you have to be comfortable with the idea that the process can sometimes contradict itself. Actually, to believe in the 'one way' to be creative goes against the very core of what creativity is.

In other words: the lack of 'a framework' in this book is deliberate. You may actually say that the lack of framework *is* the framework.

When you encounter a feeling of contradicting messages within this book, do not try to 'solve' the contradiction. Instead, reflect on how each of the contradicting messages resonates with you and what lessons they can teach you. Embrace the paradoxes to expand your understanding by seeing creativity from many sides.

And feel free to disagree or discard some of the messages presented below because they do not resonate with you. **The purpose of this book is not to teach you what creativity *is*, but to inspire you to better understand what creativity is *to you*.**

A book on creativity should not be like other books on creativity

There are thousands of books published on creativity already. To add one more, one should make a conscious decision to make it different from all the books already published. This book is part creativity book, part travelogue – you will gain insights into creativity while joining me on the journeys that brought me those insights. This decision was not just made to make the book different, of course. **The primary reason was to mix insights into creativity from a diverse set of people from all over the world, and to let the reader feel that they become part of the exploration and discovery that the author has been on for more than two decades**. When researching this book, I could spend one week in the tranquil country of Bhutan, only to find myself in the global metropolis of Singapore the following week and in a traditional German village the next. To me, that is what exploring means. Read this book in the same spirit. Do not feel pressured to read this book in a linear fashion, and definitely *do not* read it as a manual or an instruction book. All chapters can be read on their own. See this as an invitation to explore the content in a way that works for you.

Welcome to *The World of Creativity*.

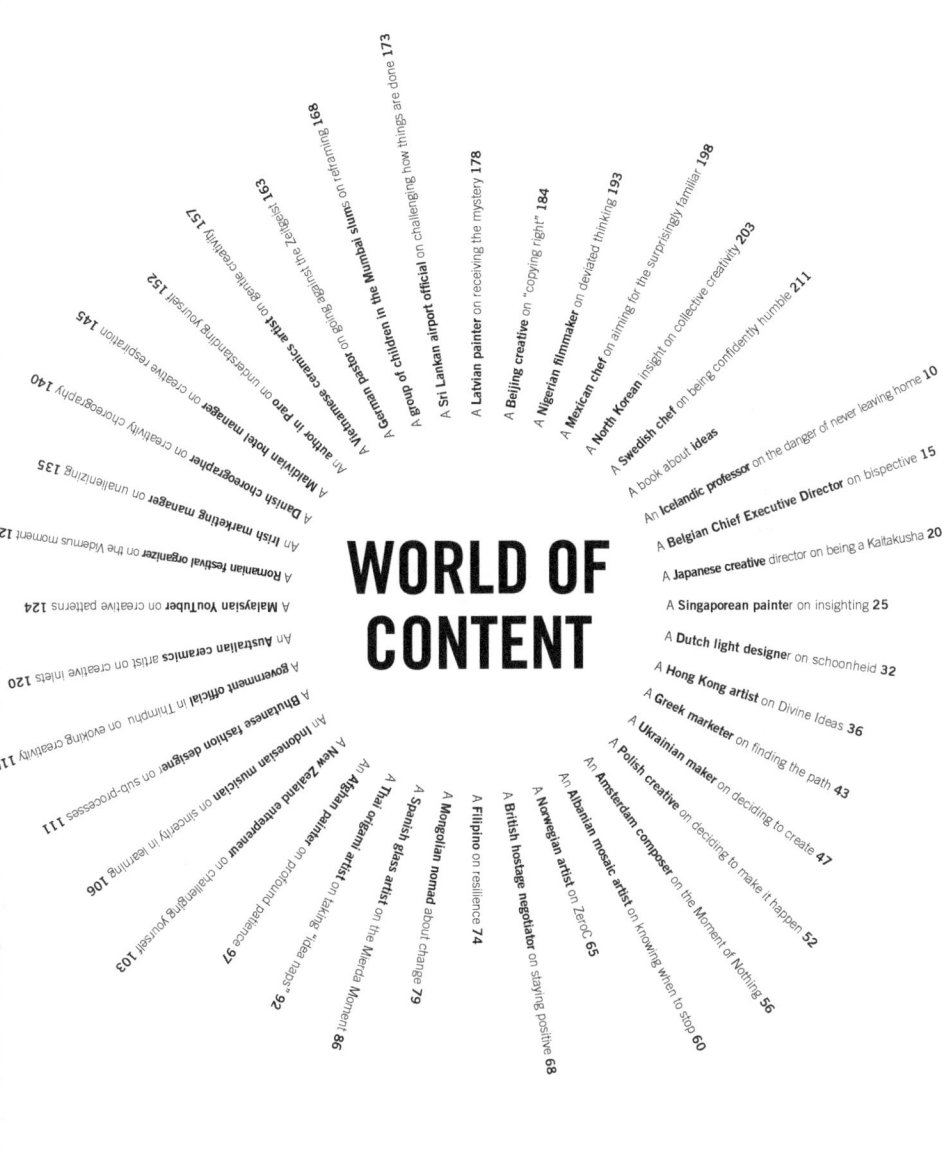

WORLD OF
CONTENT

Becoming a creativity explorer

Before we embark on this expedition into creativity together, I want to share the backstory as to how I became The Creativity Explorer. The road to writing this book has been long and winding, and it started back when I was a child. *If you are not interested in the backstory, then skip straight to the next chapter*.

I grew up in a very creative family.

My father was, as mentioned earlier, a musician and a music teacher. He played many different instruments, from the saxophone, the clarinet and the flute to the guitar and the drums, to mention a few. And whilst my brother was blessed with perfect pitch, I, unfortunately, was not. I really *did* try to learn how to play an instrument, but never got very good at it. To be honest, I sucked.

So, I grew up in a family where creativity was important and celebrated – but I did not think I was very good at being creative.

In school, I wanted to study something that would get me a creative job, so I thought I would end up in advertising, as at the time, that was where people who wanted 'a creative job' often ended up. But there was a problem: I could not draw or design, so art director was out of the question. I could not spell (this was before spell-check was a thing), so I could not be a copywriter, and I was quite disorganised, so I could not be a project manager. All the doors into advertising were shut for me. I was drawn to creativity, but could not find a path to practise it.

Luckily for me, I went to university at the same time as the internet took off. I decided to write my university thesis about 'Internet and Marketing' and because virtually no one else knew anything about the internet – this was mid-1990s – I was in high demand as an 'internet expert' because I had studied the internet for 10 weeks . . . I ended up co-creating an internet consultancy company and both the company and I thrived. I had found a place where my creativity could be expressed. The 1990s were an extremely creative time in business, and because no one knew how the internet was 'supposed' to be used, we just had to try things out.

After five years as an internet entrepreneur, we sold the company, and I decided to dedicate the rest of my life to one thing: Creativity. **My mother, who spent her whole life as a teacher, instilled in me a hunger for learning, so once I had made up my mind to try to understand this magical force that is human creativity, I decided to study it wholeheartedly**.

Since the year 2000, I have been researching the topic, interviewing people, writing multiple books on the topic and giving more than 2,000 speeches to more than a million people. My book – *The Idea Book* – was included in 'The 100 Best Business Books of All Time'.

In 2005, after becoming 'Speaker of The Year' in Sweden, I decided to broaden my perspective by moving to China.

When I arrived in Beijing in the winter of 2005, I knew no one in the country. I had no colleagues, no contacts and no friends. I was very much alone. I also did not speak the language, and I knew very little about the culture. I had moved to China on a whim, so there had been very little time to prepare or do research. After a few weeks of living there, I, of course, started to build a network of new connections, and soon I had a wonderful social network with both foreign and Chinese friends and colleagues.

But those first few lonely weeks in China changed me forever, because during that time I was in 'cultural no-man's-land'. My Swedish identity felt so distant in this Asian supercity that it rapidly faded away, and I had not yet started to embrace the Chinese way of doing things.

When I would arrive in a local restaurant, I could not read the menu or talk to the waiter, so I ended up just randomly pointing at three dishes, knowing that I probably would not like one of them, but that I could eat the other two. When the food arrived, the waiters, who also could not talk to me, would often serve the food to me with a fork, a knife, a spoon, a Chinese soup spoon and two chopsticks. They had no way of knowing how I preferred to eat the dish, nor could they ask me. I also had no clue about how one was 'supposed' to eat the dishes I was served; I had no one to ask. So, I had to look at all the different pieces of cutlery and ask myself: 'How do you, Fredrik, want to eat this?'

It was so liberating.

For what felt like the first time in my life, I had to make my own decision about how to live, behave and eat, based on what I wanted – not what my culture told me to do. The self-leadership expert Andrew Bryant likes to say: 'When we are born, we are "framed". We are given a nationality, a culture, often a religion, and sometimes a favourite sports team. That frames our thinking. This framing very much dictates what we are going to think about something'.

We think what we think are our thoughts, but they have often just been handed down to us.

A friend of mine who used to teach in Hong Kong would ask his students, 'Do you think Hong Kong was better off being ruled by the Chinese or being ruled by the British?' The class's answers were usually more or less evenly distributed between the two options. Then he would ask: 'How many of you have a different view than that of your parents?' Usually, no one would raise their hand. Their views on Hong Kong were not really their views, they were their parents' views.

It was there, at that restaurant in Beijing, that I decided that to fully understand creativity, I would have to study the topic across all countries, across all kinds of cultures and industries, all kinds of professions and all kinds of points of view. I realised that this was the only way to get to the universal truths about the topic and not to be blinded too much by my own cultural biases. Sitting alone at a table in a country where you do not even speak the language or know what you are eating will give you an 'empty mind' ready to be filled. And I opened myself up to the study of creativity.

My motto became:
To understand humanity through creativity, and creativity through humanity.

And I became 'The Creativity Explorer'.

Since then, I have talked to thousands of people to gain a deeper understanding of this fascinating topic. The more I learn, the more fascinating the topic becomes.

This book is my attempt to share some of this fascination with you.

Why we should become more creative

The energetic serial entrepreneur Johan Staël von Holstein once told me, 'Fredrik, what is the most beautiful human feeling?'

I replied: 'Love'.

Johan agreed as he enthusiastically replied, 'Yes! You are right, love is the most beautiful human feeling. But what is the second most beautiful human feeling?'

I let him answer his own question as I felt he had something he wanted to tell me.

'Creativity!', he almost screamed, 'the act of having an idea, and of making ideas happen is the best feeling in the world, bar love'.

And I think Johan is on to something.

The joy of having a truly exceptional idea is an unbeatable feeling, only beaten by being in love. When a creative revelation comes to us, we, for a moment, feel total clarity and bliss.

Creativity is what makes the world better. By identifying and solving problems, our world improves. Not only that, creativity also makes us happier and more alive.

Considering how valuable this human ability is, both literally and figuratively, it's actually rather surprising that more people do not invest more time, energy and resources into becoming more creative. I am glad you invested in learning more.

My Inner Theme – my mantra that drives me – is: **Humanity to the Power of Ideas**.

This means that I believe that if everyone were given the opportunity to reach their full creative potential – and were encouraged to pick up the best ideas from others – the world would be a much better place.

Having picked up a book about creativity, something tells me that you, too, are a big fan of this subject.

If you are ready, let's begin our journey into The World of Creativity, and let's start by diving into the topic of curiosity.

The first creative continent: The foundation of creative thinking

Core mental mindsets for creativity.

Curiosity

This is what I believe: The key ingredient in the delicious dish that is human creativity is curiosity.

Yes, highly creative people might be brave and unafraid of making mistakes, they might dream big, and they might take risks and care less about what other people think – and a thousand other things they do different from less creative people. But after having interviewed thousands of people about their creative process and spoken to more than a million people about the topic, I can say with certainty that the most important trait of an extraordinary creative person is that they are curious.

Curiosity feeds creativity.

So, let's start with exploring the topic of curiosity with insights from around the world. And let's do it for two reasons:

Reason number one: To help us better understand this intriguing human trait.

Reason number two: To get you curious about thinking about something from a global, human perspective.

This book is more than anything written to get you more curious about the world and to let that curiosity help you develop your creativity, so what could be better than to start with a story about perhaps the most curious person I have had the pleasure of interviewing: Mr. Frank Stephenson.

Frank Stephenson is a truly global soul. He is the son of a Norwegian father and a Spanish mother; he was born and grew up in Morocco and before graduating from high school, he also found himself living in Turkey and Spain. Frank has an American passport, speaks four languages fluently and now lives in England. He is also one of the biggest icons within the car design industry, perhaps best known for being the man behind the design of the award-winning rebirth of the MINI Cooper. In total, he spent 11 years at BMW, including holding the position of Chief Designer, and he was also Director of Ferrari-Maserati Concept Design and Development, headed design at Fiat and Lancia and was appointed the Head of Centro Stile Alfa Romeo design as well as Design Director at McLaren Automotive. Right now, he is designing eVTOL aircraft for the new flying taxi segment. His CV is long. And impressive.

I sat down for two hours to talk with him about creativity and curiosity. He began by saying: 'I am the most curious person I know'. His answer made me curious, so I asked him to share a story about how his mind works.

Before I share his beautiful story of curiosity with you, I want to encourage you to – as you read the story – reflect on how Frank's curious mind works and what we can learn from that.

The story begins with a stuffed sailfish.

After leaving his job as Director of Ferrari-Maserati Concept Design in Italy, but before starting his job as Design Director at McLaren, Frank decided to go on a vacation to the Caribbean. As he checked in to his hotel he noticed a stuffed sailfish behind the receptionist. He got curious and decided to ask: 'What's the story with the fish?'

The receptionist unenthusiastically replied: 'I don't know … No one has ever asked …'

The fish had probably hung there for years, but no other guest had ever inquired about it.

Frank did. Because that is what curious minds do.

And he also insisted on learning more about the fish.

Most of us wouldn't.

The director of the hotel came and told Frank that the sailfish is one of the fastest fish in the sea. Intrigued, Frank started to ask questions to learn more about this sports car of a fish. At the end of his vacation he was getting ready to fly home and start work at McLaren, but on the flight home he realised that he had not seen a live sailfish, so he got off the plane in Miami and took a taxi down to the Miami harbour to, hopefully, get to see a live sailfish. He was so lucky that a boat came in with a newly caught sailfish. Frank went up to the fisherman and said: 'Congratulations on the catch. I want to buy your fish; how much do you want for it?'

The fisherman laughed and replied: 'It's not for sale'.

Frank did not give up and replied: 'Come on, this is America, everything is for sale ... How much do you want for the fish?'

The man replied: '$20,000'.

Frank picked up the credit card that he had just received from McLaren and bought the fish for $20,000 ... (He told me that the finance people at McLaren had called him to ask what he bought and when he replied: 'A fish ...', he almost got fired before even starting his new job.)

Frank got the fish stuffed and painted it in the colours of McLaren and then hung the sailfish in the design studio to remind the people working there that they should design fast things.

But this is not a random story about a sailfish; this is a story about how being curious about a stuffed sailfish led to faster cars. Frank did not just hang the fish in the office as decoration; instead, he decided to put the stuffed sailfish into the wind tunnel to understand why this fish is so fast. There they discovered that the sailfish's scale creates small vortices that make the fish surrounded by a bubble of air instead of denser water. Inspired by this, Frank and his colleagues at McLaren designed similar scales on the inside of the ducts that lead into the engine. This increased the engine's efficiency by increasing the volume of air going into the engine by 17%. McLaren got a slightly faster car because a man on vacation got curious when he saw a stuffed fish behind a receptionist, which triggered him to want to know more.

Let's dissect this story of curiosity. It's a story about observing your world. About asking questions, and about being persistent. Of going down the rabbit hole, but also about applying what you learn to your real-world's challenges. **And perhaps more than anything, it is about wanting to know more. To understand that you do not already know everything.**

I think the story Frank shared with me is a beautiful example of the power of curiosity.

As I studied creativity and curiosity around the world, I came to realise that different languages have different words for curiosity. Words that in different ways stress the various aspects of the concept. **We can think of it like different 'dialects of curiosity'. By learning about these differences, we get a more profound understanding of what curiosity is. Or what it could be.**

For example: In my native language of Swedish, 'curious' is called *nyfiken*. *Ny* means 'new' and *fiken* means 'to have a lively and attentive desire for something'. So, the Swedish word for curiosity stresses the need to passionately pay attention to what is new to you.

In contrast, the Icelandic word for curious is *forvitni*. From for- ('before' or 'forth') + vita ('to know') which can be interpreted as 'Eagerness to know beforehand'. Icelandic frames curiosity as looking ahead to gain knowledge, an urge to know something in advance.

In Chinese culture, curiosity is more connected to the art of being interested in the unusual. In Chinese, curiosity is 好奇 (*hàoqí*) made up of the characters 好 (*hào*) 'to be fond of' + 奇 (*qí*) 'strange, rare'. So, in Chinese, they stress the fondness for the strange and the enjoyment of what is out-of-the-ordinary.

Each of these examples illustrates the many nuances that are hidden in the word curiosity. But perhaps the most beautiful etymological treasure that is hidden within a word is the etymology of the word 'curious' itself.

The root word for 'curiosity' is *cūra* **meaning 'care, attention, concern'.**

So, a poetic interpretation could read: 'That which you are curious about is that which you care about'. And the opposite is also true: 'That which you care about is what you will be curious about'.

Let me share an example. I met my wife on a blind date. At the time, I had been on many blind dates in a short period of time, and I would lie if I said that all of them had been interesting. But when Elaine walked into the restaurant, she was stunningly beautiful, and when she started to talk, she was smart, interesting and funny. Suddenly, this was not just another blind date. This was now a date I cared about. I became curious and I started asking questions. Our first date was five hours long as we kept wanting to know more about each other.

We will be curious about the things we care about, so if we want to become more curious it follows that we should make sure to care about more things and to pay more attention to the things we really care about.

The fact that you are reading a book about the nuances of the creative process that can be found around the world shows that you care about the creative process, which indicates that you are curious about the creative process – which means you are curious, which, in turn, is a great sign for someone who wants to become more creative.

Reflection

The Bulgarian word for 'curious', which is *Lubopiten* (любопитен), is made up of the word (*lyubya*, meaning 'to love') and the word (*pitam*, meaning 'to ask'). **So, the Bulgarian word for being curious reads 'for the love of asking questions', stressing the power of asking.**

I learnt about *Lubopiten* when I was being interviewed about creativity by a Bulgarian TV station. After being bombarded with questions, I turned the interview around and asked the journalist: 'How do you say the word curiosity in Bulgarian?' and he told me about *Lubopiten*.

I am so glad I asked ...

Inspired by *Lubopiten*, I'm going to give you a few questions to reflect upon:

What do you care about so much that it triggers your curiosity?

How could you deliberately increase your curiosity?

For example, for the next few days, as soon as something grabs your attention (be that an unusual design, an intriguing person or something else) make a conscious decision to stop to examine what it was that triggered your curiosity. Stay in that feeling and dig deeper there. Go down that rabbit hole on purpose. What happened? Write down your findings.

Curiosity is the key to creativity, and travel is one of the keys to curiosity. Let's travel to Iceland for both a rallying call for us to travel – and a warning for when curiosity dies.

Heimskur (Reykjavik, Iceland)

Before we dive into the topic of this chapter, let's set the scene for what arriving in Iceland can be like. The professor at Reykjavik University who had invited me to give a speech to his students had asked me what else I wanted to do during my visit to his country. I had answered as I always do when I get questions like that from my clients: 'Surprise me. I want to do something unusual'. The morning before the speech he took me swimming in the ocean where we – literally – had to move huge ice floes out of the way before we could get into the ocean. He swam around with the ice sheets for several minutes. I dipped my cold body in the ice-cold water for probably 45 seconds …

Taking your speaker swimming is not what your average Economics professor would do, but then again, **Iceland is not your average country. Far from it.**

If you have never been to Iceland, it's hard to fathom how different the country is. A small island, with a tiny population fewer than 400,000, situated just south of the polar circle. Iceland's geographical position adds to its uniqueness, nestled as it is between two tectonic plates on the edge of the European plate and the edge of the North American one.

During my trip there, I also visited the Viking World Museum, a modern glass building that looks like it landed like a spaceship on the barren Icelandic landscape. The highlight of the museum is the Viking ship 'The Icelander' (Íslendingur) – a full-scale Viking ship that visitors can even climb up on. There I learnt about the history of the Vikings and their connection to Iceland. The Vikings were the first to settle on Iceland in the year 874, and as early as 930, they established the 'Althing', one of the very first parliaments in the world.

One of the cool things about Iceland is how connected today's Iceland is to the Vikings, for example, in their language. Modern Icelandic is the closest relative to the Old Norse that the Vikings spoke, and an Icelandic person of today can, without too much effort, read the old Icelandic stories, like the Sagas, that were written more than 500 years ago.

It was during my research into the Icelandic Vikings that I came upon the word *heimskur*.

Legend has it that if you were an Icelandic Viking and you owned a farm, your job was to build a ship, gather some men and sail south. And what was the purpose of these trips? Yes, to plunder. To steal. But not only to steal gold, silver and other treasures. You were also supposed to steal ideas.

'How do they farm in Denmark?' 'How do they build ships in Norway?' 'How do they make weapons in England?'

While it was important to steal things, it was even more important to steal ideas.

If you did not do that, if you did not travel out into the world for new inspiration and ideas, then you were a *heimskur*.

Heimskur means 'idiot' ...

The first part of the word – *heim* – is Old Norse for 'home'. So, in other words: A person who never leaves their home is an idiot ...

Heimskur is a beautiful word for a beautiful insight: If we do not venture outside of that which we already know we will not become wiser.

As I was swimming with ice sheets with my client, I was reflecting on how refreshing it was to have a client who took me ocean swimming in the middle of winter, instead of just taking me out for dinner. I must have been to thousands of dinners with clients. Now, there is nothing wrong with a dinner, but swimming in the North Atlantic Ocean is clearly more memorable. His creative idea inspired me to be more unexpected in how I treat my own clients and suppliers. Ice bathing might have constricted my blood vessels, but it opened up my eyes. And my mind. **Travelling is truly the antidote to complacency.**

Finally, an interesting observation. According to Auður Ava Ólafsdóttir, an Icelandic author and history professor, Icelandic is the only language that uses the same word for 'home' (*heima*) and 'the world' (*heimurinn*). How beautiful is that? They literally build a connection between the place we live (our home) and the world we live in. Icelandic entrepreneur Hjalmar Gislason expressed it beautifully: 'Our world is our home, and our home is the whole wide world'. So while we become stupid for never leaving our home, we should still look at the whole world as our home. It is in this apparent paradox that the true wisdom lies.

Reflection

Many of today's companies – and today's people – are *heim-skurs*. They only look for new ideas within their own company, their own industry or their own well-known world. They do not venture out.

The way to cure this sickness is to force yourself into unknown environments. If you work for a car company, do not go to yet another automotive show. Instead, go to a hotel and tourism conference to get some fresh ideas about how the hospitality industry is developing new ways of keeping its guests happy and then implement them in your showroom. If you work for a five-star hotel, go to a car show and learn how the mobility industry is tackling user experiences that might trigger some new ideas for your hotel.

In other words: Do not be a *heimskur*.

Do not be an idiot.

Identify an area where you are at risk of being a *heimskur*. First, define your 'home base' – the habits, processes or procedures that feel so natural to you that they risk making you 'blind' to other ways of doing things. Then, deliberately focus on where you could travel to gain new perspectives on how to do those things. **Finally, and this is the hardest part: make sure you actually go there and get those new perspectives. Just thinking about travelling is not travelling ...**

Curiosity has many dimensions. Iceland brought us Heimskur – a message about breadth in curiosity. Next, we go to Brussels to learn about "bispective" – a message about depth in curiosity. While both are important, the second one gets much less recognition. Time to change that.

Bispective – the unique competence of being able to see something from both perspectives (Brussels, Belgium)

A person (Person A) who has worked in an advertising agency her whole life has a lot of experience in creating advertising. She has a certain perspective on advertising. Another person (Person B) who has worked in a marketing department her whole life has a lot of experience in commissioning advertising campaigns. She, also, has a certain perspective on advertising.

But a person (Person C) who has worked both in an advertising agency (creating ads) and in a marketing department (commissioning ads) has the unique competence that comes from seeing the creation of advertising from both sides.

Person C has a 'bispective' on advertising.

Bispective is a made-up word created by combining the Latin word for 'two' (bi) with the word 'perspective' where 'spec' means 'to observe'.

So, a person who can look at a situation from two perspectives has a 'bispective'. Bispective is different from simply having empathy. To have bispective you need to have actual experience of both sides, not just the ability to imagine being on the other side.

Here are some other examples of expertise that will generate bispective:

- A salesperson who previously worked as head of procurement, who can now understand how people who buy his services think.

- A person who becomes a parent and who can now understand both how it feels to be a child, but who can now also take the perspective of a parent.

- A former lobbyist who switches sides and becomes a politician, and who can now better understand the struggles of politicians trying to make their voters happy.

Having bispective is like having two eyes instead of one. A person with just one eye loses some ability to perceive depth, and a person with just one perspective on something loses the ability to perceive depth of understanding in that area.

I learned about bispective from Margit Kunz, Chief Executive Director at the German-Belgian-Luxembourg Chamber of Industry and Commerce.

A chamber of commerce always has bispective. They represent their home country (in Margit's case, Germany), but they also represent the local market in which they work (in Margit's current case Belgium and Luxembourg). I met her for the first time when we both lived in Singapore.

In her previous life, Margit has worked both as a public relations professional for a local theatre as well as a local journalist. Working both in public relations and journalism gave Margit 'bispective' on media.

According to Margit, having bispective gives a person many advantages:

(1) You can better anticipate different outcomes, and you work on them much faster.

(2) You become more empathetic towards your counterpart and can more easily see their point of view.

(3) You gain the ability to play through different scenarios and look at a situation from different angles.

And she then added: **'And on good days it allows you to be more open-minded – you become less confrontational.** You can more easily respect the other side, and it becomes easier to change your initial plan or your strategy when you are wrong'.

After having been a professional speaker for 20 years, I was once tasked to organise a conference for professional speakers. Suddenly, I found myself on the other side of the 'booking a speaker-table'. I thought I understood the process of booking a speaker – after all, I had been booked as a speaker more than 2,000 times; but when I was the one actually booking the speakers, I suddenly looked at the process in a totally new way. Getting frustrated with speakers for not submitting their slides on time, made me appreciate the patience of meeting planners. Having speakers requesting many changes to the schedule, length of speech etc., made me aware of the need for speakers to be more accommodating. Hearing speakers ignoring the brief I had given them, made me promise myself to always pay full attention to speaker briefs, and so on.

Organising a conference for speakers, made me a better speaker to work with for conference organisers because now I had bispective on the speaker booking process.

Most people speak just one language, but, according to the *Journal of Neurolinguistics*, 43% of the world's population is bilingual, utilising two languages daily.

A person who is bilingual not only knows how to speak two languages but being bilingual also increases creativity, flexibility and open-mindedness – and might very likely help one have better cultural awareness.

Just as the world is becoming aware of the advantage of speaking two languages, we also need to become more aware of the huge advantages of people having bispective on what they do.

The more I hear about bispective, the more I realise that it's the opposite of an extremist.

Extremists tend to dismiss or reject alternative viewpoints, show strong resistance to nuances and prioritise ideology over evidence. They often view the world in binary terms as in 'us vs them'. **A person with a bispective mind, by definition, will automatically think in alternative viewpoints.** Will easily see the nuances of their area of expertise and think in terms of 'us and them' vs 'us vs them'.

A bispective mind is a very powerful tool. Having bispective makes you more curious, less judgemental, more open-minded and more empathetic – and, of course, gives you a broader perspective: all things that help you become more creative.

Reflection

Identify as many examples as possible of situations where you have, or have had, a bispective. Write down all the benefits each of those bispectives gave you.

In which area would you benefit from gaining bispective? Identify what the opposing skill would be that would give you a good bispective. Write down what you need to do in order to get that. Make a plan to add one more bispective to your life.

Seeing two sides of a story is what bispective is all about. Seeing the future, while understanding the present, is what "kaitakusha" is all about. It is perhaps the ultimate bispective. Let's find out why.

Kai-taku-sha – One who cultivates the frontier (Tokyo, Japan)

The Japanese have given us some wonderful concepts related to creativity. Like *Kaizen* (改善), the art of continuous improvement. Or *Wabi-Sabi* (侘寂), the beauty in imperfection and transience. And *Shoshin* (初心): Meaning having a beginner's mind.

I would like to introduce you to another one: *Kaitakusha* (開拓者), which translates to 'someone who cultivates the frontier'.

I learned about *Kaitakusha* from Kyoko Yonezawa, Head of Innovation at TBWA\HAKUHODO in Tokyo. Kyoko runs the Innovation Hub at TBWA\HAKUHODO where she and her team explore the latest developments in technology to find new ways of pushing the boundaries of marketing and advertising for their clients.

Kyoko is a Human–Computer Interaction specialist, so she is an expert on the intersection between humans and machines.

I asked her how she looked at the concept of 'Human Innovation Interaction', a concept I just made up for our discussion and by which I meant the understanding of how to best get people to develop and adapt to new ideas.

She laughed and said: 'In general, people are supportive of things they are already used to, things that they already know. Change is very difficult for most people'.

But she then went on to emphasise the importance of having people who try new things: 'Without people who cultivate the frontier we would stagnate. We would go extinct'.

I asked Kyoko what the mindset of a Kaitakusha is, and she gave me the most poetic reply: 'You know the saying

"If you want to go fast, go alone
If you want to go far go together"

But do you know how it ends?

"If you want to go fast go alone
if you want to go far go together
If you want to go above, convince others to fly fast
with you"'

This is the essence of a *Kaitakusha*. It is not just pushing the envelope. **No, a *Kaitakusha* is going to the edge of the known to plant and harvest new thoughts and ideas that we can bring back to the rest of her group.** Thoughts and ideas that will bring the others along towards the new.

Kaitakushas bring people closer to the future. They settle in the new.

In English, we have the word 'pioneer', but it doesn't quite capture this spirit. This is especially true if you keep in mind that the origin of the word pioneer is the French *pionnier* meaning 'foot-soldier' or 'pawn'. Pioneers were the soldiers who were first sent towards the front. Pioneers were cannon fodder.

The Japanese word *Kaitakusha* with its meaning of 'someone who cultivates the future' is not only more poetic and beautiful, but also points to the creation of the people who are *Kaitakushas* as they bring back the 'harvest' from the future.

They do not just 'explore' the new land. They cultivate it.

Kyoko gave three short and concise rules to follow if you want to be an effective *Kaitakusha*:

(1) Do not be afraid.

Do not be afraid of new ideas, new technology or new innovations. But most importantly, do not be afraid of the people who bring you these new ideas.

Remember: Approach the new.

(2) Find the benefit.

Do not just explore the new, actively try to find the value that it will bring. Search for what makes this better. For how it will improve our lives.

Remember: Harvest the new.

And then finally,

(3) Share the harvest.

A Kaitakusha is not just invested in finding the new, she is also trying to get others onboard.

Remember: Share the new.

Do not just settle on being an innovator, a trailblazer, a pioneer or (the very boring title of) 'early adopter'.

Instead, be a Kaitakusha.

Be a person who cultivates the frontiers of humanity.

Reflection

Kaitakusha sounds like a simple and beautiful concept but practicing it in real life is harder. Here are three concrete steps you can take to make it easier.

Step (1) In honour of 'Approach the new'.

Reach out to the one person in your network who is the most forward-thinking in an area that you know will become important to you. For example, who do you know who knows the most about the current AI development? Invite this person to lunch with the specific goal of getting this person to share with you the most interesting new thing that he or she has seen on the AI horizon.

Step (2) In honour of 'Harvest the new'.

Go to a website that writes about the future of technology and pick an article to read. Then read the article with the purpose of forcing yourself to find an insight around how this new tech could improve your business. If you want to challenge yourself, pick an article that, at first sight, has absolutely nothing to do with what you do, and then use the exercise to try to find a valuable insight or takeaway for your own business.

Step (3) In honour of 'Share the new'.

Step one was to find someone who could teach you something; now let's turn the table: this time you must find someone in your network who needs to know about the insight that your friend in the first step taught you. Who do you need to share your newfound insight with? Book another lunch, and this time you are the teacher of the new. Remember that an important aspect of Kaitakusha is to cultivate the new so that others benefit too.

Do all three steps and you are a true *Kaitakusha*.

Sometimes we play the role of a Kaitakusha to bring the future to others. Sometimes our peers bring us what we need.

Next, we venture from Japan to Singapore to discover the concept of insighting, for when a peer becomes your mentor.

Insighting (Singapore, Singapore)

As an author, when I read a book, I am not just enjoying the story. I am also, almost as a totally separate brain activity from the reading, analysing how the text is written. 'Why did the author use this specific word?', 'Why a comma here?', 'Why did she include the fact that the main character had glasses?' And so on.

As a speaker, when I am listening to a speech, I am not just absorbing the message, I am also, as a totally separate brain activity from listening, analysing how the speech is delivered. 'Why did the speaker start with that story?', 'What in the set-up of that joke made it work?', 'Why is the speaker walking over to the edge of the stage?' And so on.

Every creative person does this in the area they are active in. A bartender will not just walk into a bar to enjoy a drink. She will also observe how the bar is being run. A plumber will not just walk into a hotel bathroom to use the restroom. He will also think about why the pipes were drawn the way they were.

And art lovers will look at a piece of art to understand what it means to them, as well as try to understand it better by understanding the artist and will enjoy it as a creative expression there to evoke an emotion in them.

But fellow painters will look at the art piece for all the reasons listed above, but will also – as a totally separate brain activity from enjoying art – analyse the techniques used to create the painting in order to see if there is something they can learn from that which they can use in their own painting.

Writers will at this point contemplate whether my decision to repeat the phrase 'as a totally separate brain activity' is purely stylistic, or there to make a subtle point by getting writers to think about this specific question just before I mention it. (The answer is: Yes, I purposefully repeated the phrase three times to get fellow writers to reflect on that stylistic decision.)

This specific skill of studying another creative person in your own field to get insights into how or why they did what they did to create what they created is what I call 'insighting'.

It is more narrow than general curiosity.

It is more active than inspiration.

It's more focused than just studying.

I learnt about insighting from Abu Jalal Sarimon. He is a third-generation Singapore artist who grew up on a small island outside of Singapore where he would start painting with sticks in the sand. While other kids made traditional sandcastles, he studied how the crabs built strong houses with the clay from underneath the sand and he used that insight to create much more elaborate sandcastles than the other kids.

Today, he is an established Singaporean artist who is deeply involved in the local art scene. Sarimon is the Founder of Freedom & Love International Art Group, an Executive Member of Singapore Modern Art Society and Senior Member of Singapore Malay Artists of Various Resources. He works regularly as a curator across the region.

I met with him at his art studio at the Goodman Arts Centre, a quiet oasis in the otherwise often bustling city of Singapore. The studio is so covered with art – from floor to ceiling – that it was hard for us to get a seat where we could talk.

Sarimon shared with me how he, already as a kid, would think differently than the other kids: 'For the other kids a book was just a book to read. For me, it was more than a book. I was looking at the design, I was looking at the material, I was looking at the way the author wrote, I was looking at the thickness of the book. For them it's a book – for me it's beyond a book. I kept asking questions: "What is the author trying to show? What is he trying to share?", "Why did they choose this kind of illustration?" and so on. When you read a book in this way there is a lot of 'Why?', a lot of questions. **For people who think this way there is a hunger. A hunger to understand'.**

And now, as an adult and an established artist, Sarimon still has this hunger to understand why something was done in a specific way.

This act of wanting to understand how and why something was created – what I choose to call 'insighting' – is what triggers inspiration, but it is important to understand that the act of insighting comes before the inspiration. You either choose to do it or you don't.

Creative people choose to do it.

Because they need to know how something was done.

When asked how to approach insighting, Sarimon explained: 'Try to identify the uniqueness of the creator. An apple is an apple, but every painted apple is different. Observe the apple that this painter created and try to figure out what he or she did to create the uniqueness of that apple'. Sarimon would do that by creating, what he calls, 'layers'. He will talk to the artist, to the curator and to other artists who are attending the exhibition to get as broad a perspective as possible around how a painting was created and why. He wants to understand things like choice of materials, why the artist went for a specific texture, the choice of colours, the painting technique and a million other things that will give insights he can then use for his own future painting.

Insightings are insights that you can only pick up by studying a fellow expert in your own field. For some creatives this does not come naturally. Sarimon: 'Many artists are lonely people. They are on their own. They do their own thing. Many do not mix with others. And many are insecure. They are suspicious and think you are going to steal their ideas or their style. So, I create these meeting opportunities where I invite them to open up, and to share their knowledge. Share their skill. Allow them to learn from others'.

According to Sarimon the key is trust. People will not share their insights unless they trust you. So, if you want to get insightings you first must build trust with peers.

Sarimon is an artist who has understood the value of learning from peers. Be it by hanging fellow artists' artwork in his studio so he can study it, or by working as a curator to build connections with other artists who will open up to him and share their knowledge, or by him helping organise regional exhibitions to make new connections with more artists. It's all done to increase his chances of getting more and better insightings from other artists.

'I ask (fellow artists about their work) because I want to learn. I want to understand the process', he told me. 'When you see something good, always ask. Always listen. Have a positive mindset. And always be ready to receive insights. It will drive you to learn more. To create something that is better'.

Reflection

I will give you two things to reflect on.

First: Identify a process where you practice insighting today. It should be a practice that you have where you are subconsciously studying a process to understand it while doing something else. Like how I, as an author, reflect on the way a text is written even as I read it.

Second: Identify three peers whom you respect and admire, but whose creative process you do not fully understand. Then contact one of them per week and invite them to share something about their process that they feel is important for a fellow practitioner to know.

The second creative continent: Exploring the creative process

On this continent we will be looking at a few of the specific moments that can be found within the creative process that have not gotten the attention they deserve.

Schoonheid: Beyond beauty (Amsterdam, The Netherlands)

When a programmer writes a flawless line of code, it is called 'beautiful code'. When a footballer makes an exceptional pass, it is a 'beautiful pass'. A perfectly crafted argument is a 'beautiful argument', and an elegant solution to a math problem is a 'beautiful solution'. In these moments, 'beauty' describes creative perfection in its simplest, most natural form.

But the Dutch have a word that goes even deeper: *schoonheid*.

While the English word 'beauty' traces back to the Latin *bellitas*, meaning 'pretty, handsome, charming', the Dutch word *schoonheid* stems from *sconi*, meaning 'clean', 'pure', 'bright' – and 'something beautiful'.

***Schoonheid* conveys a sense of profound purity and clarity that transcends mere aesthetic appeal.**

When we strive for creative excellence, we should aim for ideas imbued with *schoonheid* – ideas that resonate with purity and brilliance, because those ideas have the highest chance of being our most valuable. To get these ideas we need to understand that ideas can come to us in two ways: the Eureka Moment, when we feel we've found a great idea, and the Mevrike Moment, when a profound idea finds us.

Eureka is Greek for 'I found it', while *Me Vrike* means 'It found me'. The Mevrike Moment is quieter, calmer and more serene – but also more profound. It's in these moments that we encounter ideas filled with *schoonheid*.

These are the ideas that, instead of exciting us with a burst of energy, bring us a sense of calm and awe – like the quiet wonder of seeing a firefly. Fireflies, by the way, are a perfect metaphor for *schoonheid* ideas: clean, pure, bright. And beautiful.

I learnt about *schoonheid* from Daan Roosegaarde, a modern Dutch artist whose creations are filled with this profound beauty. Just as Dutch painters of the Golden Age were fascinated by light, Daan uses the purity and brightness of light to create works of art that are more than beautiful – they embody *schoonheid*.

Some of Daan's recent projects include SEEING STARS, in which city lights are turned off to reveal the night sky; SPARK, an organic fireworks display using bubbles and light, and the SMOG FREE PROJECT, the world's first outdoor air purifier that turns smog into jewellery. Google them to get a visual understanding of what *schoonheid* looks like in practice; they are stunning and really need to be seen, not just described in words.

In our conversations, Daan shared that true creativity involves surrendering to your ideas. While the creative process requires effort – trials, errors and execution – it also demands stillness, openness and a willingness to invite *schoonheid* into your life.

So how can we attract *schoonheid* ideas? According to Daan, it is about cultivating an environment and mindset that welcomes ideas. It requires an energy that is unthreatening, egoless and fully present. Like how one attracts a firefly.

One of the times I was interviewing Daan, he was, fittingly, working on the world's largest Firefly Garden in Bali, helping to restore the magic of fireflies lost to light pollution.

Reflection

In chess, beginner players are often given the advice: 'Do not move until you see it'. That means that one should not play a move that just 'feels good', but one should wait until one sees that one correct move. The right move to play. The beautiful move.

Apply the same advice to your creativity. **Do not settle on an idea just because it feels 'good' – or worse, feels 'good enough'. Wait until you feel that the idea is the one.**

Aim for *schoonheid* – the pure, the bright and the clean solution.

Or to be more precise: aim to put yourself in a state of mind and in a physical and mental environment that will facilitate that you will be creating ideas that are more than beautiful. Ideas that are full of *schoonheid*. Do a '*schoonheid* check-in' when you are in the middle of creating to make sure you are in the right frame of mind and not just rushing to finish or settling on a lesser idea.

Understanding that ideas find us, not the
other way round, is worth two chapters.
One from a Western perspective. One with an
Eastern. Both with a human perspective.

Let's fly from the Netherlands to Hong Kong
to meet the divine.

Mortal Ideas vs Divine Ideas
(Hong Kong, China)

Here is one of the most fundamental things people get wrong about ideas: They think there is just one kind of idea. They, incorrectly, think that we 'get ideas from our mind' and thus there is just one way of coming up with ideas.

The truth – as any truly creative person will tell you – is that there are two ways to get ideas, and these two ways are so fundamentally different that it is a deficit of the English language that we use the word 'idea' to describe both of them.

To separate the two, let' us call them: Mortal Ideas and Divine Ideas.

Mortal Ideas come from our conscious mind. Those are the ideas where we feel that we 'come up' with something. Where we feel that 'we' are being creative. Divine Ideas are the ideas that come to us, where it feels like we are being given a gift. Where it feels as though we are just a vehicle for something bigger.

This definition of 'Mortal' and 'Divine' ideas comes from ceramic artist Johnson Tsang from Hong Kong. I met with him in his studio at the Jockey Club Creative Arts Centre, an old, worn down, high rise that hides studios for all kinds of creatives, from dancers to fashion designers. Behind a very inconspicuous yellow door at the end of one of the many hallways lies Johnson's studio. It is a studio full of wonderfully creative ceramic art.

It's hard to describe some of Johnson's creations, but here is an attempt at some descriptions: a human face that opens up to reveal two other faces kissing. A human face that has become a pillow where a child is sleeping peacefully. Or a canoe made out of a human face, and so on. I hope you get the picture. (If you want to see these and other works of his, I recommend you check out his art; he is @johnson_tsang_ artist on Instagram, where he, by the way, has more than 600,000 followers, so clearly, I am not his only fan.)

These hyper-creative art pieces are the result of what Johnson calls Divine Ideas. Divine Ideas are ideas that have come to him during sleep, intense relaxation or meditation. **He does not look at these ideas as ideas that he has 'created', instead he looks at them as ideas that have been given to him 'as a gift'.**

A gift from something divine. (To be clear, not necessarily a gift from God, but a gift given by 'something larger than ourselves'.) An idea that is not 'from us' but instead something we feel that we have received.

The history of human creative brilliance is filled with examples of Divine Ideas. From Buddha sitting under the Bodhi tree to John Lennon saying how the song 'Imagine' came to him 'fully formed' or mathematician Henri Poincaré explaining how ideas 'presented themselves' to him. Beethoven is said to have said: 'Music comes to me unbidden – I must give it to the world'.

It is exactly this sense of 'receiving a gift' that Johnson is referencing with his categorisation of some ideas as Divine Ideas.

Johnson said: 'I think that those ideas (the Divine Ideas) were not mine. When I'm doing meditation, or dreaming, sometimes I get those ideas from there. It seems as though I go into a very different world and then over there, there are many, many ideas floating. I just raise up my hand, and then I can grip any ideas'.

Johnson Tsang estimates that 70% of his creations are the result of Divine Ideas, ideas that have come to him in dreams or in meditation. What about the other 30%? Those are ideas that come from his conscious mind. Johnson calls these 'Mortal Ideas' because these ideas are 'merely mortal'. There is nothing divine about them. Mortal Ideas are ideas that we create by ourselves. Johnson again: '(The Mortal Ideas come) from my training, from society, education, the people around me, things happening around me'. (To see an example of a 'Mortal Idea' of his check out: https://www.instagram .com/p/C_VHpn6hX3F/ and I think you will easily see the difference between his Mortal Ideas and his Divine Ideas.)

Now, here is an interesting observation: as I was walking around in his studio observing his art, I could point at a piece and say 'This is a Mortal Idea' and then point at another one and say 'This is a Divine Idea' and *every* time I was correct.

The Mortal Ideas were nice, funny and cool. There was nothing wrong with them, but something was missing. The Divine Ideas were stunningly different and intriguingly unique. Divine.

The creative process for Divine Ideas and Mortal Ideas is very different.

Johnson: 'Mortal Ideas come from my brain and are about the society – how I feel about the world around me, my actual feelings. They are something I respond to in society or something present. I just try to use my point of view to tell a different story. Divine Ideas are something I cannot control'.

Learning from Johnson Tsang, the following distinctions between Divine Ideas and Mortal Ideas became clear:

> *Divine Ideas: come from somewhere else.*
> *Mortal Ideas come from ourselves.*

Divine Ideas express a universal idea through us.
Mortal Ideas is us expressing ourselves.

For Divine Ideas we are just a vehicle.
For Mortal Ideas we are in charge.

For Divine Ideas you feel like you received it.
For Mortal Ideas you feel like you created it.

To receive Divine Ideas you are passive.
To have Mortal Ideas you are active.

Divine Ideas (usually) arrive fully (or almost fully) developed.
Mortal Ideas are (usually) slowly developed over time.

Divine Ideas come when you are empty.
Mortal Ideas come when you have a strong feeling or
opinion about something.

So how do you know when you have had a Divine Idea? It is a bit like saying 'How do you know when you are in love?' **If you do not know whether you have had a Divine Idea or not, then you haven't had one, but when you do have one, *you will know*.**

Personally, I know just what Johnson Tsang means when he talks about Divine Ideas. The most powerful idea I have ever brought to the world came to me in a dream. I woke up at 2 a.m. in a hotel room in Thailand after having the most beautiful nightmare. I dreamt a story about how there exists an invisible human race on Earth. I essentially dreamed a movie. The whole story came to me, including mood, facts, names of characters and much more. Before that dream, I had never thought about writing a novel, now I was sitting in my bed in the middle of the night at a random Bangkok hotel and said to myself: 'This story has to be told'. The story I dreamt became the novel *The Unvisible* and came out on Penguin. The whole time I wrote the book, I never said to myself, 'What should I write now?' Instead, I said to myself: 'Let me know what happened next'. I felt that I was just a vehicle for the world I had been given. When the book was about to be published, I even told the publisher that I did not want my name on the cover, or that if we had to have my name on it, it should say: 'As told to Fredrik Haren', not 'By Fredrik Haren'. Unfortunately, the publisher did not let me do that, but so strong was my feeling that the story of *The Unvisible* was not 'created by me' but 'given to me'. Not by a 'god', but by something. Something Divine. If someone reads *The Unvisible* and tells me that they 'love it', or that they 'hate it', I do not take it personally. After all, it was not 'my' idea. It was given to me.

And here is something very interesting: at the end of my interview with Johnson Tsang he said: '**A Divine Idea is something you cannot control, it's like you are getting a message, and the Divine Ideas always have a message of love.** It's a pure world, full of love, there is no fear, no hatred, no fight, no war, no anger. When you get a Divine Idea, you feel happy and blessed. I always work with on a smile on my face when I work on a Divine Idea. It feels like I am still in a dream when I work with them'.

This description seems true for anyone who has received a Divine Idea. These ideas are pure and universal, positive and good.

Understanding the powerful essence of Divine Ideas, it will come as no surprise to anyone that when asked which ideas Johnson Tsang thinks are the best, Divine or Mortal, his answer is just a big glowing smile.

We should all aim for more Divine Ideas. It would make the world more beautiful.

Reflection

If you have never had a Divine Idea, it might feel disheartening to hear about its power and beauty. And when you learn that they arrive as a gift, it might seem impossible to do anything to increase the chances of them coming, but according to Johnson Tsang you can increase the likelihood of Divine Ideas gracing you with their presence: '(If you want Divine Ideas,) stay calm. Give yourself some time to be quiet. Give yourself more time Work in a quiet place, spend more time alone. Meditation is the best method. Everyone can do it – when taking a bath, going to the toilet etc'.

So, that is the activity for this chapter: Schedule a receiving session.

Find a quiet and serene place and close your eyes and start to meditate to invite the ideas to come to you.

This is no guarantee that a Divine Idea will arrive, but it is a guarantee that you have started a process that has drastically increased the chances of them coming to you when they feel that you are ready.

And if you have received a Divine Idea, think about what you can do to increase the percentage of ideas you get that are Divine. Johnson Tsang's long-term ambition is to be in a place where he only works on Divine Ideas. That is probably very hard to achieve, but it is a beautiful ambition we should all aim for.

Divine Ideas are what we should aim for, but the path to get there is not to aim anywhere, but to just find the path.

Let's voyage to Greece to find out how.

Find the path (Athens, Greece)

If you ask a group of people to define what an idea is, one of the most common answers is: 'An idea is a solution to a problem'. It might be a common answer, but it misses a core aspect of creativity. An aspect that I was inspired to learn from during a conversation with Greek marketing expert Natalia Symeonidou. Natalia currently works as Chief Marketing Officer (CMO) at a Greek IT company. Her career also includes a 15-year tenure at the advertising agency McCann Worldgroup, culminating in her position as Head of Strategy.

When I asked her for her own definition of creativity, Natalia told me: 'What I understand, creativity is a process of getting somewhere – even when things don't go your way'.

What I love about Natalia's definition is that it focuses on the journey – not what might stop it. After all, problems, of course, are not what we want, but defining creativity as a 'solution to a problem' is still not right. **What we want is what's beyond that problem.**

Creativity is a path.

A path to greatness.

'The problem' is just a metaphorical stone lying in front of us, stopping us on our journey to that greatness. Finding a way around that metaphorical stone is not the end goal; what is beyond that stone – the path – is.

When you look at creativity as a path to explore, just like Natalia does, the creative process becomes more joyful. Natalia: 'I believe that creativity has a lot to do with optimism.

The only way to be creative is basically to believe that there is a way, and that's what sets creative people apart from non-creative people. Creative people are those who, when you tell them something, they'll say, "You know, just let me think about it and let me figure something out". The non-creative people are the people who will say "There is no way we're gonna to be able to do this"'.

But creativity is more than *just* optimism. It is not just hopefulness and confidence about the future or the success of something; it is going out there to make it happen because you know that the path is there. You can be optimistic and just sit on a stone, but that is not going to create anything. You need to follow the path.

If you are focused on finding the right path, a stone will not stop you. It will just make you think about an alternative path to get around it.

I asked Natalia how to adapt a mindset of 'path finding' and she said: 'The first part in finding the path is to have the inherent belief that there is a path. Often in the creative process you have to walk into the fog and only when you take the next step can you see what lies beyond, but when you believe that there is a path you're also not afraid to fail. Creativity has a lot of trial and error. Error does not mean failure. It basically means that you need to take another path, and you've learnt something valuable from whatever error you made'.

Think of being creative as trying to escape from a maze: When you start you have no idea how to get out, and the only way to get out is to try different paths until you find one that works. Going down a dead-end is not a 'failure' when you are trying to get out of a maze – it's a way to find out that that specific route was not the right way out, and now you have one less dead-end to explore so you are closer to getting out. You keep trying to find the correct path. But for this to work you must believe that there is a path.

The trick, according to Natalia, is 'To be optimistic and to be kind - mostly to yourself - and very forgiving. And by forgiving, I don't mean that you make excuses, but I mean that you don't take the whole thing personally. You approach obstacles with curiosity. Just explore this path of creativity and have the confidence in yourself that somehow, you'll make it. Even in the darkest hours, believe that you will make it'.

Believe that there is a path.

Reflection

Select a current creative challenge you are working on. Instead of focusing on the problem you need to solve, identify five different paths you can take in order to reach your goal in a beautiful way. Map out the path with a focus on how to move forward, not on the obstacles on the way.

Finding the path is a way of thinking about creativity, a positive conviction that a solution exists, but no ideas will see the light of day if we never decide to make them happen.

Time to visit Ukraine to talk about doing.

The Facite Moment (Kyiv, Ukraine)

I once heard a story about a bunch of Western Europeans and a Ukrainian who were in a car that broke down in the middle of nowhere. The Europeans tried to call for help, but there was no mobile reception. They got out of the car and walked around to try to get better coverage, but to no success. They were at a loss for what to do next. When they got back to the car again the Ukrainian had already repaired it ...

This, to me, is a good description of the people of Ukraine, whom I have had the pleasure of learning from during multiple trips to the country. They are doers. They fix things. They get things done. It is with great sadness I watch this beautiful people and country be bombarded by Russia for no logical reason. But the way in which Ukraine has fought back against its much larger attacker is inspiring to say the least.

One of the Ukrainians I have had the pleasure to get to know is Yuri Vlasyuk. Yuri is the epitome of a doer. He is the founder of makerhub.org and the chairman of the board of the Ukrainian Maker Association. He has dedicated his life to building meeting places where people can come to learn and be inspired to make things. To build a community of builders. Before the war they had 15 Maker Fairs in 5 Ukrainian cities. At Makerhub all kinds of makers meet and learn from each other; everything from beekeepers to robotics builders to people experimenting with propane gas, and beginners figuring out how to use a saw. Yuri and his team are trying to create an atmosphere that democratises technology and makes people less afraid of it.

His mission is to get more people to do more things, to create and make things with their hands. He calls it the

'antidote to learned helplessness' and explained to me: 'When your instinct is to just buy a new item when something breaks, you lose something. You become a little bit helpless. But when we get people to build things, what they really build is trust. And confidence. If you feel that you can fix something you build resilience'.

Resilience is the word that describes Ukraine during the war.

When the war started, Yuri refocused his energy from getting kids and adults to create their own fun projects, like building their own LED lamp or fixing a computer, to helping build a network of makers who build things that would help them defend their country, like parts for home-made drones.

Listening to Yuri talk with passion about the joy that people get from making things, it became clear that there is a moment in the creative process that is more powerful than the Eureka Moment, and that is the moment when someone decides to create something.

Let's call that moment 'The Facite Moment'. *Facite* **is a Latin word meaning 'do', 'make' or 'create'. It is a direct command or encouragement similar to saying 'Do it', 'Make it happen' or 'Get it done'.** A message from your mind to tell you to actually do something. It is not when you have the idea. It is when you decide to make something happen. A 'motivational expression that strongly implies active participation, creativity or productivity'.

Please note that the Facite Moment is an irresistible internal force. It pushes you to make something. It's different from deliberately choosing to act on an idea, which we will read about soon.

Without the Facite Moment – the moment when you decide to make something – ideas would not come true.

As a 'super maker', I asked Yuri for his own experiences of the Facite Moment. He said: **'It's like a voice inside me telling me that I just have to do something. It's like an invisible hand that pulls me towards whatever I feel I have to create next. When I feel that, I cannot resist. I do not want to resist'.**

He paused for a while, as if to reflect on the power he had just described, and then he said: 'This force, I can't compare it to any other feeling ...' He smiled. And then he added: '... or perhaps the moment I met my wife'.

A lot of people think that creativity is about 'having ideas'.

It is not.

It is about making ideas happen.

It is about making things.

It is about creating.

The -ing at the end is important. It defines an act of doing.

The most powerful moment in the creative process is, arguably, the moment when you feel the force pushing you to make an idea come to life. Learning to recognise this feeling when it comes, and to be able to harness the energy that is there, is one of the most important skills for someone wanting to be creative. And finally: It is a skill. Meaning, it can be taught, trained and improved.

Reflection

When was the last time you felt an internal voice inside you tell you: 'You have to do this'?

What did that feel like? Put words on it. Write down the description of how that felt. **Just like a diary can help us understand ourselves better, in the same way, writing down our feelings and reactions to the creative process can help us understand our creative selves better.** And understanding how we feel when The Facite Moment strikes can help us become better at both recognising them and taking advantage of them.

If the Facite moment is about responding to an internal force, then the To Kano moment is about making a conscious decision to make an idea happen. They are very similar, yet profoundly different.

To master creativity, we have to understand both, because sometimes we are pulled into making our ideas happen, and sometimes we need to be the ones pushing.

The To Kano moment: The moment when you decide to make an idea a reality

As someone who writes about creativity, I've come across countless ideas and concepts that have the potential to change the world. However, the real magic isn't in the idea itself – it's in what Iwona Fluda, an award-winning serial entrepreneur, digital artist and founder of the Ministry of Creativity LLC, would call 'the To Kano Moment'. Iwona grew up in Poland – a land of doers – and has since grown into a global creative (we met up at a café at the Zurich train station where we were transiting to new destinations). The phrase 'the To Kano Moment' is inspired by The Eureka Moment. But while the Eureka Moment describes the moment you have an idea, the To Kano Moment describes the moment you dedicate yourself to make this idea happen. **To Kano is Greek for 'I make it happen'. It's that critical moment when you stop dreaming and start doing, transforming your wishful thinking into 'doful thinking'.**

Iwona thrives at the intersection of creativity, science and technology, and her approach to life is all about making things happen. In our conversation, she shared, 'People do not think they can make it happen'. This is a powerful observation, and I think she's absolutely right. So many great ideas never see the light of day because we get stuck in the thinking phase. We dream big, but when it comes to execution, we, so often, falter. Iwona described how she, in her creativity workshops, would give the participants 'homework' to practice on making an idea happen. She estimates that more than 90% of the participants do not accomplish the task. They cannot even make an idea happen when they have been assigned to do so.

Iwona proposes three ways to overcome the inertia of not starting an idea: develop self-trust, scale it down to a manageable task and get going. I love this because it's so practical. Creativity is not just about coming up with ideas but about having the confidence to execute them. Self-trust is essential – believing that you have what it takes to see something through. Then, breaking it down into something smaller and more manageable takes away the intimidation factor. And finally, getting going – practise the art of starting things.

This brings me to an intriguing concept that ties in perfectly here: the Doing Quotient (DQ). Unlike IQ, which measures cognitive abilities, or EQ, which measures emotional intelligence, DQ is the intelligence of getting things done. Some people are clearly more intelligent than others, and in the same way, some are better at making ideas happen. DQ is about the ability to execute, to think not just 'What could be?' but 'How will we make this happen?' People with a high DQ do not just talk about their ideas; they act on them. Personally, I would much rather invest in a person with high DQ than someone with high IQ.

Iwona Fluda, in my opinion, has an exceptionally high DQ. At the end of our interview, she asked me, 'How can I help you?' When I mentioned that I wanted to speak more in Africa, she didn't just nod politely or say she'd get back to me later. Right there and then, she picked up her phone and connected me with people in five different African countries who could help make that happen. This is what having a high Doing Quotient looks like in action – thinking and acting on opportunities in real time.

For Iwona this is important: 'We need people to go from "wishful thinking" to "doful thinking". Think about how to get it done, not what you wish would happen'. It's a mindset shift from passivity to action, from pondering to creating. The world is filled with wishful thinkers, but what we really need are doers – people who understand the art of getting things done. As she poignantly noted, 'We need to teach the art of getting things done in schools'. Imagine a world where children are not only taught to dream big but also given the tools and confidence to act on those dreams.

One key takeaway from my conversation with Iwona is the importance of getting started on your ideas as close to the moment you have them. **The energy of a new idea is like a spark – it's at its brightest and most powerful when it first ignites. If we wait too long, that spark dims, and the chance of taking action dwindles.** The 'to kano moment', preferably, needs to happen soon after the 'eureka moment' to keep that momentum alive.

As much as we should celebrate the Eureka moment and the wonderful power of having a great idea, we should celebrate even more the To Kano moment—the moment when someone decides to make their idea happen. Because that is – frankly – one of the most powerful moments in the whole creative process. Creativity is not about having ideas – it's about making ideas happen. And the moment you decide to do just that is even more powerful than when you had your idea.

Reflection

When was the last time you decided to make one of your bigger ideas a reality? Try to go back to that feeling when inspiration turned into dedication.

And the next time you decide to run with an idea, pause and marvel in the To kano moment. Get energy from it. And send a grateful thought to the skies for gifting you with the power to make ideas happen.

We go from covering one important aspect
of the early stages of the creative process
to another. We leave Zurich and
travel to Amsterdam.

The moment of nothing (Amsterdam, The Netherlands)

When does the creative process start? That is a harder question to answer than it seems. It could be said to be when we first identify a problem, when we collect inspiration and knowledge or when we have our Eureka moment. All those answers are correct, but then there is another way of looking at it: The creative process really begins at the Moment of nothing – one of the most beautiful moments in the creative process that too many people totally miss, rush past or are oblivious to.

I learnt about the Moment of nothing from Sebastiaan Roestenburg, a music composer and producer who mainly creates commissioned work for brands, agencies, film and advertising.

According to Sebastiaan the Moment of nothing is a fleeting moment just before we go into creation mode.

It was when Sebastiaan described his creative process that he, in passing, mentioned the Moment of nothing. Sebastiaan creates music for a living. For example, advertising agencies will send their commercials to him and commission him to write custom-made music for those ads. He will watch the ad, read the brief, set up his piano and recording equipment, turn off his phone and sit down at his piano to start writing music. And just before he puts down his first finger on the key to play the first note, Sebastiaan pauses for a second. *That is the moment of nothing.*

The moment when all the preparations have been done, but no creation has started. A moment when anything is possible, all roads are open, where you can go in any direction – but have not taken the first step.

Sebastiaan: 'It is where you are prepared to create, so everything is there, everything is set up and you feel "Now I'm going to start working. There's a moment of nothing"'.

According to Sebastiaan this is a good moment. He said: 'To me it feels like a lucky moment. Nothing is there, so everything can be created'.

But at the same time, it is a scary moment. Sebastiaan again: 'It also feels a bit maybe ... insecure. It's a bit dangerous maybe, or not dangerous, that is not the right word, but it can be an insecure moment, because you're also not sure if it will happen or if you will be able to create something really great, which you have in your mind. And it can also be a disappointment afterwards'.

The Moment of nothing is that split second before you start to create. It's like the moment just before a diver jumps off the board. The moment just before chess players raise their hands to grab the first piece. The moment just before a painter puts the first brush stroke on the canvas.

It is the moment just before you jump into the rapid river that is creation. After you have taken the plunge, you can never go back. The process has started. You have taken off.

The Moment of nothing is full of human potential. Infinite hope and possibilities. Endless choices. It contains the promise of total success, utter failure and everything in between. And it has so much built-up energy.

Sebastiaan compares it to kinetic energy. He said: 'The energy is built up, but it's not released yet. It has yet to come out'.

Since Sebastiaan is a musician, I asked him to write me a jingle that would symbolise the Moment of nothing. I wanted to hear what this moment sounded like to a person who thinks in music. He sat quietly for a while, reflecting on my request, but then replied: 'It has no sound. It is just quiet'.

Of course, the sound of nothing is nothing. I should have known.

Treasure this 'calm before the creative storm' that is the Moment of nothing. Skipping over it, or ignoring it, could seem like no big deal. But welcoming the Moment of nothing is just the kind of thing that separates truly creative people, such as Sebastiaan, from the rest. They might not do it consciously, but they do it. **Mastering creativity is not about being good at doing creativity exercises, it is about understanding all those small magical moments that make up the creative process, like the Moment of nothing.**

Reflection

For one of your future creative projects where it would make sense, schedule the recognition of the Moment of nothing for just after you have set everything up, but right before you start to create.

Then – at that split second – close your eyes, take a deep breath, pause and stay in that moment. Make the moment last. Then open your eyes and use the energy that acknowledging the Moment of nothing gifted you to jump-start your creation.

When you are done creating, go back to that moment and reflect on how it made you feel.

To reach our creative potential, we need to master how we start – but also when to end. Skipping the Moment of nothing is a missed opportunity, and missing the Tetelestai moment has ruined many ideas from reaching their greatness.

We are off to Albania to learn from a man who has inserted millions of screws, nails and staples, but whose job is to know when to stop.

Tetelestai – To know when to end
(Tirana, Albania)

'When do you know when to stop?', that was the question I ended up discussing with mosaic artist Saimir Strati around a small, round table at a quaint café in Tirana, Albania. Saimir looks just like someone a casting director would cast as an Albanian mosaic artist. He has a big, curly head of hair and a salt and pepper beard. His clothes are in the style of a person who doesn't care about clothes. But what you really notice about Saimir is his eyes. He has the eyes of someone who doesn't just use his eyes to see, but to observe.

Saimir started his mosaic career restoring mosaics in the Albanian historical sites of Apollonia, Amantia and Byllis, and he has since ventured into a variety of mosaic techniques. He has created some stunning work. Like how he spent almost a month building a mosaic of Mother Teresa out of 1.5 million (!) brown and white staples, a feat that got him into the Guinness Book of Records. Or how he created a portrait of Leonardo da Vinci out of about 500,000 industrial nails.

It was this portrait of da Vinci we were discussing when I asked him how he knows when he is done. **This question of 'How do you know that a creative project is done?' is a universal question.** Knowing when to stop is a crucial question to ask for an editor editing a text, a musician putting notes on paper, a president writing a speech or an architect sending away the drawings to the constructor. But the hammering in of hundreds of thousands of nails like Saimir Strati does is the perfect environment to understand the act of finishing a creative project. How would you know that you are done when you hammer in the 497,543rd nail? Why not stop at 497,542? Or continue to 497,544? That is why I wanted to discuss it with a mosaic artist like Saimir.

Saimir looks at the creation of an art piece as a communication between artist and artwork. Saimir: **'First I choose what to create, but as time progresses the piece is communicating to me'**.

According to Saimir the aim of a creative person is not to aim for 'perfect', but to aim for 'balance' – the balance between the energy of the artist trying to realise his or her vision and the energy of the creation that, in lack of other words, has a life on its own. An energy that will surprise you in a positive way and push you in unexpected directions.

Floating in this place between perfection of the vision and the life of the creation, Saimir puts in one more nail, and then another one, and another one.

And another one.

And one more.

And one more.

And one more.

And then, suddenly:

Peace.

The universe just tells him: It is done.

A moment of peace.

Of balance.

It's at that very same moment that the editor puts down her pen. That the musician closes the piano lid. That presidents tell their speech writers that their speech is done and that architects send their blueprints off to the builders.

According to Saimir Strati that is when he says 'goodbye' to his mosaic. It's like the art piece moves on. That moment should feel clear, obvious and apparent. There should be no doubt.

Knowing when to stop, at the right time and for the right reasons, is crucial for making amazing ideas come to life.

If the Eureka moment is the welcoming of an idea, then this is the bidding farewell to an idea. This very special moment needs a name.

May I propose: *Tetelestai*.

Eureka is Greek for 'I found it'.

Tetelestai (τετέλεσται) is Greek meaning 'It is completed' or 'It's done'.

The Tetelestai Moment is the moment when you feel that your idea is completed. (According to St. John, *Tetelestai* is, by the way and fittingly, the second to last word of Jesus on the cross.)

Of course, there are some instances where a creative project will be re-developed, like how the decorating of a room is never fully finished. We tend to go back and re-visit our decoration choices after a while and add a vase, or remove one, or redesign the room from scratch after a few years. But that is different. That is about looking at a creative project over a longer period of time.

The editor might revisit a text and find a missed spelling mistake and update the blog, a musician can try to play the piece of music in a different way than it was written, the presidents might change their delivery in the moment on stage and the architects might change their design after the builders give feedback after construction has started.

But the Tetelestai Moment is the end of a specific creative process. The completion of that creative task. In Saimir's case: that moment when, suddenly, adding one more nail would ruin the beauty that has been created.

Saimir Strati calls the Tetelestai Moment a moment of peace. Peace in the mind of the artist, but also peace within the artwork itself.

Reflection

To notice this moment of peace is a skill – let's call it 'completion awareness'. Like other skills, it can be trained.

A lot of focus has been given to the art of *starting* the creative process, like how people are encouraged to paint the first brush stroke or write the first word to get going. But much less focus has been given to teaching people to know when to stop. To say goodbye to one's creation.

As you come to the end of your next creative project use the finalisation of that project to practise completion awareness.

Prepare yourself for the Tetelestai Moment by paying attention to how your mind behaves as the end of the project is near. Observe yourself. Check your state of mind to be sure you are ready for the silent whisper – or perhaps violent screaming voice – that is telling you that you are done.

We leave Albania and the message of finding peace to finish in peace. We land in Norway to discover a different kind of peace: the peace that lies in completion.

Zero Creativity (ZeroC) (Oslo, Norway)

Einar Sandvold, is the kind of artist who is not making art to make a living. He creates art to survive. It's a way for him to make sense of the world and to, temporarily, create a sense of normality in his mind. Einar's creative process is intense. He can stay up all night to paint, to put on canvas the chaotic thoughts in his head. His mind, as so many minds of creatives, is constantly spinning with questions, reflections, issues and ideas.

But there is one moment when his mind calms down. It is the moment of Zero Creativity (ZeroC). **ZeroC is the rare moment of complete creative emptiness that occurs right after you have finished a creative project, but before your mind starts spinning about the next one.**

Einar: 'Those minutes right after I have put down my brush and my painting is done, I feel relief. That's when I feel my mind finds a temporary sense of calm. It's creative weightless-ness. Total bliss'. Then he added, 'Then the thoughts rush in again'.

Einar shared how there is virtually always a voice in his head showering him with things to think about, often hard and heavy thoughts. Einar suffers from frequent panic attacks, and his art is a way to deal with these thoughts. But when he enters 'ZeroC', right after finalising a creative project, then – for a brief moment – that voice in his head is gone. And nothing else takes its place. It's then that he just sits down, with his cat, or with a cigarette, and treasures the calm noth-ingness that is ZeroC.

ZeroC is something that many creative people can relate to. They often share how their mind is more or less constantly bombarding them with ideas and problems to solve. It's what drives their creativity in many ways. But that voice can be exhausting to listen to. To not lose their minds they need a break from these constant bombardments.

Call it a creative ceasefire if you will.

Einar: 'It (ZeroC) works as a reset. It resets the system. Clears the mind. Unplugs it. Then it's off again to the next creative struggle'.

And that is why ZeroC is so important to be aware of. So that you can cherish the temporary peaceful silence of the mind that comes with it.

It's a reset.

A reset that we need.

Reflection

The next time you finish a creative project, be aware of the arrival of Zero Creativity, because ZeroC is like a shooting star. Beautiful as it stops you in your tracks and makes you be in awe of the universe and forget about everything else – but then gone in the blink of an eye, just as quickly as it arrived.

It would be a shame to miss that moment of bliss.

The third creative continent: Positive challenges and creative breakthroughs

Mindsets and approaches to help with creative development.

A hostage negotiator's technique of using positivity to stay creative

Suzanne Williams is an experienced hostage negotiator who has worked on some of the most high-profile and dangerous hostage situations across the world. When she was at Scotland Yard, she was the most senior-ranking officer in charge of both the Kidnap and Hostage Negotiation Units. She is now an Associate Fellow at Oxford, and she also works as an independent crisis and hostage consultant. Over a 27-year career as a hostage negotiator, she has worked on hostage situations involving more than six hundred hostages. She has talked to Al-Qaeda, negotiated with sea pirates off the coast of Africa, with environmental activists and many, many other hostage takers around the world.

One day, she took the time to talk to me.

About creativity.

I asked her what the job of hostage negotiator was like, and she said, **'It's a job that only someone who is comfortable with uncertainty can do. It is very unpredictable. There really is no script'.**

Suzanne went on to explain that most of the time the negotiator knows very little about the hostage taker, and a big part of the job is to try to find out more about them, who they are, what they care about, who – and what – could influence them, what drives them, etc.

Her job is about finding the chinks in the armour that she can use. A big part of her job is about looking for clues about who the people on the other side are. She is constantly looking for hooks that she can use against them. To find 'the magic formula that is going to unlock a specific situation'.

And she has to find out as much information as possible from someone who is not very keen on sharing any information at all.

So how does she do it? And what can we learn about the creative process from these extreme situations?

Suzanne Williams told me about the importance of asking questions ('If you do not ask questions you do not learn anything new'), about the need for empathy ('You really have to be able to put yourself into the shoes of the other person') and about the ability to practice active listening ('You have to understand to be understood').

And then she shared something with me that I found so very interesting.

She said: **'Sometimes there is a lot of negativity. You have to block that out or it's going to interfere with your creativity'.**

To be creative you need to decide to block out the negativity? I asked her to elaborate, and she said:

'You must stay positive. Do not let the bad guys win, and make sure you remain in a positive frame of mind. What I physically have to do is to filter out negativity, but I also have to filter out any of my own bias and prejudice. I have to filter out my own experiences. I cannot have a (negative) pre-convinced assumption about how it is going to end; I have to clear my mind. If I do (have negative preconceived assumptions), I could not do my job. And bad people will win, and good people will not be allowed to go home'.

What? 'Filter out any previous experiences?' I was confused.

'But would that not take away all the advantages of having 27 years of experience', I asked.

Suzanne clarified that it is not about blocking out all your previous experiences – but to filter out all the previous *negative* experiences.

She explained that we need to block our negativity in order to be able to be creative. **To be able to see the possibilities.**

Remember, she is dealing with situations that are extremely stressful, hostile and uncertain, or as she put it: 'It's human misery. People die'. Hostage negotiations are no walk in the park, and people who go to such drastic measures are not in a good place.

Suzanne's approach is not about sugar-coating the situation or to be naive – it is about being on an active lookout for some positive possibility that could turn a dire situation into a happy ending.

Because there is often very little information and very big stakes involved, there are usually not very many positive things to go on, so she needs to be in a state of mind that makes it possible for her to find that one sliver of hope, or for her to see that one faint possibility.

It could be some possibility lurking within the culture she is dealing with, the location where the hostage situation is happening, an anniversary that is coming up, a stakeholder who has a potential way in. And her job is to find it.

In the words of Suzanne: 'Make sure your mind is open enough to pick up anything positive'.

Her words really resonated with me. **She seemed to argue that we can only find what we are looking for, and we will only go looking if we think we can find it.**

She said: 'You have to stay positive. Do not let the bad guys win and remain in a positive frame of mind'.

And it is true: Creativity really is to look for positive opportunities. It is about actively searching for positive opportunities. Very often when we need to be creative it's because we are facing some kind of problem or challenge. Hopefully not something as dramatic as a kidnapping, but still things that require us to handle and solve one of the many curveballs that life throws at us. Situations where we need new, fresh ideas to fix it. In situations like that negativity can be a burden.

Reflection

The next time a problem is demanding your creativity, keep Suzanne's approach in mind. Make a conscious and deliberate decision to push away all the negative judgements, prejudices and experiences that might block you from seeing that one possibility that can take you out of your misery and solve the problem.

First: Write down all the negative thoughts and assumptions you have about your project. All the reasons why it will not work. Acknowledge that you have those negative thoughts.

Second: Write down all the possibilities and opportunities that you see. All the things that could go right.

Third: Go back to your list of negative assumptions and rewrite each of them into a lesson to remove the negativity.

Fourth: Go back to your list of possibilities again and try adding more to that list.

Remember: **This isn't just naive optimism – it's professional possibility-seeking and focused opportunity finding.**

The journey around the world of creativity takes some unexpected geographical turns. From a hostage negotiator in England, we just learned about why we need to filter out negativity in the moment to tap into our creativity.

Next we proceed to the Philippines to learn about what will help us sustain a high level of creativity over time. That story, perhaps surprisingly, begins in a flooded street in Manila in the middle of the night. It is a story of resilience.

The joy of resilience (Manila, The Philippines)

It's 2:38 a.m. in Manila and a rainstorm has flooded the road to Tagaytay. What had been a road is now a little lake, and the water reaches the belly buttons of the people brave enough to check how deep it is. In one of the hundreds of cars that are stuck, my driver, fittingly named Joy, is laughing.

I look out at the other people around me, and I see three children, they cannot be more than ten years old, having a blast in the makeshift swimming pool that their road has become. Did I mention it's 2:38 a.m.?

I see men on motorcycles getting soaked both from the rain and from the flooding, and it seems all of them are in great spirits. I see taxi-drivers, lorry drivers, rich and poor stuck in their jeepneys or their SUVs, and they are smiling too. There is literally not a frowning face to be found.

It is in this precise situation I understand what the world can learn about creativity from the Filipinos. **The lesson is about happiness and its connection to resilience and about how resilience can help you be creative.**

That Filipinos are a happy people is a well-known fact, but where does this happiness come from? The answer to *why* Filipinos grow up so happy eluded me even though I am married to a Filipina and have spent countless hours in the land of laughter. But then I met Jo-Dann Darong, or JD as he is commonly known, and he pointed me in the right direction.

JD is Director III at the Department of Trade and Industry of the Philippines, and one of his responsibilities is to develop the creative industries in the country.

He told me: '**We are brought up to see the silver lining.**
Remember, we are a country with 24 active volcanoes, more
than 7,000 earthquakes every year and numerous typhoons
hitting the country each season. We have also been invaded
by three countries (Spain, the United States and Japan) and
have been occupied consistently for three hundred years until
we finally got our independence a few decades ago. In short:
There are many negative stories we could tell ourselves.

But instead, we tell ourselves the positive stories'.

JD exemplified with how his grandmother, who lived during
the Japanese occupation, never told stories of the hardships,
instead she told stories about how they managed. About how
they survived. Stories of resilience.

If you grow up hearing stories of hate, hardship and struggles,
you become bitter, hateful and hard. If you grow up with stories
of resilience and positivity, you become positive and happy.

Resilient might mean someone who is 'able to withstand or
recover quickly from difficult conditions'. But the word 'resilience' is more than just being able to withstand or recover. The
true meaning of the word is 'the act of rebounding or spring-
ing back', from *re-* meaning 'back' and *salire* meaning 'to jump,
or to leap'.

To be resilient is to bounce back. Not just to come back – but
to bounce back.

And the people who can bounce back are the people who tell
themselves the positive stories.

Many people think that the ability that creative people have is that they dare to take risks or that they are not afraid to fail. But I would say that they have the ability to bounce back after failure. That they go back and try again.

Creative people are resilient. And resilience comes from telling yourself the positive stories.

After sitting in a car for 30 minutes, Joy turns to me and says: 'Sir, I think we can drive on now'. I look out of the car and see that the temporary lake is still surrounding our car and there is no way I would have driven anywhere if I were the driver, but I trust Joy because of her driving skills and because of her attitude. She fires up the car and starts to drive. The water reaches over our tyres, and the car creates tiny waves as she pushes through. Joy turns on the radio and starts to sing as she is creating another positive story – not about how we got stuck in a flood in the middle of the night, but about how we pushed through and made it to our destination, despite getting stuck in a flood.

Reflection

What stories are you telling yourself? Specifically, what stories do you tell yourself about the times when your creative projects did not go according to plan? Are they stories of failures or stories of resilience? Stories about not succeeding, or stories of bouncing back?

Here is a practical thing you can do to see how changing the story you tell yourself changes the way you think: Think back to a recent time when you 'failed' at something creative and then write down a description of how you failed. Then adopt a mindset of resilience and write one more description of what happened but *only* write down the positive effects of what happened or what it led to.

As a speaker on creativity people often want to tell me how they believe that 'creative people are not afraid to fail'. **The more I interview creative people, the more convinced I am that the most creative people are very unconcerned with the concept of failing. They are focused on creating, and they are focused on going back to creating when things did not work out. So is that not 'not being afraid to fail'? No, it's 'being focused on bouncing back'. The first is defensive. The second is proactive.**

The people of the Philippines reminded us to use
resilience to bounce back from setbacks.
The nomads of Mongolia will now remind us to
move forward from success. An eighty-year-old
Mongolian on a horse will be our teacher.

Move like a Mongolian (Somewhere on the steppe in Mongolia)

The man in charge of the nomadic tribe that has set up camp next to a small mountain on the edge of the desert about a twelve-hour drive from Ulaanbaatar is more than eighty years old. No one knows his exact age. He has a name, but I just call him 'Sir'. It feels like the right thing to do. The man has an aura of self-evident authority that comes from living a long life close to nature. The lines around his eyes are deep and many, and his skin is darkly tanned. He has the face of a man who has lived a long life exposed to the extreme and harsh conditions of the Mongolian steppe. But he is also a very happy and content old man. Many of those lines around his eyes come from a life of laughter. Even at his respectable age, he still herds his animals with a long wooden stick while sitting relaxed on his horse.

I had the privilege of spending a week or so with his tribe, sleeping in their Yurts, watching them work and, more importantly, sitting around the fire at night – under a sky filled with more stars than I have ever seen – to discuss their approach to life.

I was there, together with my good friend Kevin Cottam, who is an expert on the Nomadic Mindset, because **I wanted to understand what people who live a nomadic life could teach us modern people about creativity.**

The first thing I was taught was that much of what non-nomads think it means to be a nomad is wrong. The definition of Nomad is 'a member of a people that travels from place to place to find fresh pasture for its animals and has no permanent home'. We tend to look at this definition and think 'they are people who always travel' or 'they do not have a home'. But that is wrong. As one of the Mongolian nomads told me as he pointed at the Yurt we were sitting in: 'We have a home. This is our home'. And then he added: 'And we do not always travel. We only travel until we find the perfect place to live'. When they find that perfect place, they live there for months. But – and this is the crucial aspect of being a nomad – every morning when they wake up, they stick their heads out through the door of their Yurt and say: **'This was the perfect place to live yesterday, but is it the perfect place to live today?'**

If the answer is still 'yes', they stay there for another day.

If the answer is 'no', they tear down their village and move until they find an even better place.

This openness to questioning yesterday's decisions was echoed not only in the elder's lifestyle in the nomadic village, but also in modern Mongolian thinkers like Batgerel, whom I interviewed in Ulaanbaatar. She said: 'Being a nomad doesn't mean the movement of the body. It means the movement of the mind'.

Batgerel, who, when I met her, was in charge of the branding of the country, so elegantly points out: To be a nomad is a mindset, not a physical position.

This mindset, as Batgerel described it, means letting go of attachment – not just to physical places but also to old ideas and habits that no longer serve us.

I call this mindset to 'Think like a Mongolian'. It's all about being able to move on from how one has been doing something in the past, because what was previously the right choice is now wrong.

Let me tell you a story to give you an example of how one can apply this mindset back in our modern world. This is a story that happened to my brother. When he arrived at the airport, he was asked to check in through one of these new automatic check-in machines. The machine asked him for his booking code, but each time he entered the code he got an error message. Finally, the machine gave him the message: 'Wrong code. Please contact Service Staff'.

My brother approached the lady working for the airline to get help. The lady – *without* seeing my brother's booking code – asked him, 'Do you have a 1 or a 0 in your code?'

My brother checked his code and replied: 'Yes, I have a 1'.

The lady from the airline replied: 'Try changing the 1 to a lower-case letter "L", because "1" and "l" look the same'.

It worked. His first reaction was to thank her, but then he remembered that she had actually never seen his code ... He went back to her and asked: 'You never saw my code, and yet you knew I had an "l". Let me guess, this problem happens a lot?'

She replied with a smile: 'Oh, yes, happens all the time'.

Then my brother told her: 'Then I have an idea: Why don't you call your IT department and have them remove all the ones, all the zeroes, all lowercase l's and all the uppercase O's? That way, no one will ever have this problem again'.

The lady smiled and replied: 'No, it's fine. I love to help people'.

Moral of the story: **The airline forgot to change the way this lady thought about her job. For thirty years or so her job had been 'I check people in'. But now her new job is 'I make sure people have no problem checking in by themselves'.**

For thirty years she did her job correctly, but suddenly – because of the introduction of the self-check-in-kiosks – that way of working was wrong. And she had not been able to move on. She did not move like a Mongolian.

We all need to become better at questioning our old ways before they become the wrong ways.

Kevin Cottam, the man I went to Mongolia with, has studied nomadic tribes on multiple continents and written a book about his findings (The Nomadic Mindset). He told me: 'I met a student, Binderiya, at the University of Mongolia on one of my trips to Mongolia and Binderiya said, "Nomads Think Vastly, Act Narrowly"'. Moving across the steppe makes them think about the world as big. Travelling lightly makes them focus on what they choose to do. This mix of broad thinking and laser focus is essential for nomads, but it can easily also be applied to being creative. **The phrase 'Think Vastly, Act Narrowly' works just as well as a rallying call for creatives to both be thinking big and, at the same time, be focused on the task at hand.**

The trip to Mongolia changed me forever. Climbing up on a hill in the morning to see the vastness of the steppe made me humble, while at the same time made me appreciate the ability to think bigger. To see farther. Living with the nomadic family made me see how little you need to be happy, and how calm one becomes when one lives in nature. Lives with nature. From nature. But more than anything, the mindset of 'Moving like a Mongolian' taught me the power of being able to unapologetically move on from old habits. I still remember standing on top of that hill overlooking the vastness of Mongolia and making a commitment to myself to question my 'perfect spots' more often.

I asked Batgerel how a nomad knows when it's time to move on, and she replied: 'We can sense it. We sense it in our animals. We sense it in the air'. **And I think we can all become better at sensing when it's time to move on.**

Mongolia taught me the power of being able to move on. I hope you will also learn that from them.

Reflection

Take a moment to reflect: What is one thing that you have been doing for a long time that it's now time to stop doing? Something that has served you so well, but now it's holding you back. Something that was right to do at the time but now isn't right anymore.

This, of course, is harder than it seems. People often stick with things they have done for a long time even when it is not serving them well anymore. Think of how people stay in miserable marriages long after they stopped making them happy or stay in jobs they should have quit long ago. There is a high probability that you, too, are doing a lot of things that you should have stopped doing.

To help you identify things you should change, here is an exercise that might help: Write down 10 things you do in your creative practice. It could be a process, a behaviour, an activity, a tool you use, a mentor you have, a belief you hold, etc. Then next to each, answer this question: 'If I moved on from this, what would I move on to?'. Finally, pause for a second at each answer and listen to what you feel when you reflect on if it's time to move on from that specific activity or habit. Remember the words of Batgerel: Do you sense it in the air that it's time to change?

We should all stick our heads out of our metaphorical Yurts that is our lives and ask, 'This way of doing things was great yesterday, but is this still the right thing to do today?'

If the answer is 'yes', then let's keep doing it.

If the answer is 'no', then let's change. And let's do so without guilt or remorse.

The previous chapter and the next are both about productive dissatisfaction.

The Mongolia chapter was about moving on from success. The Spanish chapter will be about using failure to turbocharge the creative process.

And while the Manila chapter was about bouncing back from setbacks, the Barcelona chapter will be about charging forward from a specific kind of epic failure.

Do not be alarmed, but the next lesson is centred around a swearword.

The Mierda Moment (Barcelona, Spain)

You often hear people say: 'We need to celebrate failure' as a solution to encourage more creativity. But a recent meeting with a glass artist in Barcelona got me thinking differently about the connection between failure and creativity. And it made me realise that most failures do nothing to boost our creativity. Many failures even kill creativity. Some can break us. But some failures nudge us forward. **And a certain kind of failure – a rare but very special breed – gives us a huge boost of energy and inspiration that will fuel creativity like few other things. I am talking about 'the Mierda Moment', and when you learn how to harness that, you too will get access to a very powerful creativity tool.**

I got to know about 'the Mierda Moment' from Anna Alsina Bardagí.

Perhaps I should start by saying that *Mierda* is Spanish for 'crap'. In other words, the Mierda Moment is not a very pleasant phrase, but it is the name of a very nice insight.

Let me give you some background.

Anna Alsina Bardagí is a woman who creates beautiful sculptures out of the purest of glass. And she does it through a process that is both intricate and painstakingly slow. One piece takes hundreds of hours to make. One mistake and it's ruined. Her pieces sell for thousands of Euros each, yet she almost gave up on the process due to constant failures in the beginning.

When I met her at her studio in Barcelona she told me how, in the early years of her art career, her art pieces would constantly break. Most of the time the failures would just beat her down. She would get frustrated and annoyed. She would lose energy.

But one specific time when she took out the glass piece only to see it cracked and ruined, she got a burst of energy. She said: 'Mierda!' (i.e. 'Crap!') and decided to once and for all figure out *why* the glass kept cracking. She spent days in the library reading scientific journals, digging deep into the physics of glassmaking. She contacted world experts in glass to learn from the masters. She started taking detailed notes about what was going on. And finally, she figured it out and invented a new way to create glass art.

The Mierda Moment is not the same as a 'Eureka Moment', which refers to 'the common human experience of suddenly understanding a previously incomprehensible problem or concept'. The Mierda Moment is a special kind of Eureka Moment that is triggered by the frustration of failing.

The Mierda Moment is also different from 'flow'. Flow, also known as being in the zone, is 'the mental state in which a person performing an activity is fully immersed in a feeling of energised focus, full involvement and enjoyment in the process of the activity'. There is nothing like the enjoyment when the Mierda Moment hits you. It's a state of flow like energy, but it is driven by extreme frustration.

And the Mierda Moment is not your average 'learning-from-your-mistakes'. It's a force, like a turbo-button being pressed in a computer game where you suddenly gain previously unseen energy to find a solution. **An energy that came from built-up frustration.**

Anna credits this extra 'energy boost' for helping her push through to a new level of understanding. Of giving her the 'push' she needed to create at a higher level. She told me: 'That one specific failure triggered something in myself that got me to do this extensive research. The Mierda Moment is a trigger. It's like a drive. It is a fearless drive to break through what is stopping you'.

The Mierda Moment is not just a celebration of failure. Nor is it merely about learning from failures. Learning from failure is just about slowly becoming better step by step, understanding what does not work. But the Mierda Moment is like this huge push. **It is about failure triggering this creative energy that propels you forward.**

If we want to be creative, then it's important to be receptive to when the Mierda Moment arrives so that we can ride that wave that the Mierda Moment creates when it shows itself. Or we might miss it.

Because, as Anna taught me, 'It's not enough to never give up. It's more powerful than this. It is the difference between successful, creative people, and unsuccessful people. It's not that creative people don't give up. It is that they use the force of the failure to push themselves forward. They use the energy of the failure'.

'It is so easy to get pulled down by failure. To think, "I failed so I am a failure"; "I will never learn this"; "I might as well give up". And then you lose your chance. You miss your opportunity to do something that you love. Sometimes you might even start blaming yourself. Or others'.

Anna shared with me that there are certain aspects that will increase the possibility of the Mierda Moment showing itself. When we work on a creative project that we are really passionate about, the added passion can transform frustration into positive energy.

Know that failure is not personal. When you distance yourself as a person from the situation that failed, you are more open to seeing positive opportunities opening up.

Never give up. In the words of Anna Alsina Bardagí: 'Keep trying. Keep trying. I think that life, our whole lives, is a learning process'. The more you look at life as one long lesson, the more open you are to learn the lesson when it shows itself.

The world of innovation is full of people who used the positive energy of something negative. From the frustrated child who kicks a malfunctioning vending machine into order, to how Steve Jobs used the frustration of being fired from Apple to build Pixar into a great company, enabling him to come back to Apple with fresh ideas.

Reflection

Remember the words of Anna Alsina Bardagí, the glass artist who almost gave up after all her art pieces cracked for the longest time: 'The lesson here is when something cracks, don't just get frustrated. Use that energy to crack the problem. **The Mierda Moment is the moment in which you harness the energy of your failure to push you forward'.**

Harnessing the built-up energy of the Mierda Moment is not something we can practise in advance. But being aware of its existence will help us take advantage of it when it does arrive. That is the purpose of this chapter: to make you aware of this force.

What we can do in advance is build Mierda Moment Readiness.

(1) Since passion, amongst other things, helps to trigger Mierda Moments, gauge your passion level in your current creative project. If it is too low, perhaps you should move on.

(2) Strengthening your Depersonalisation Mindset. Write down a recent failure. Did you write down how *you* failed, or how the *process* failed? If you wrote down how you failed, rewrite the failure to describe what failed without blaming yourself. (From 'I cracked my glass sculpture again' to 'The glass cracked for some reason'.)

Remember this chapter for the moment in the future when you fail spectacularly, but instead of feeling broken down you feel elevated and energised. Because that is when you will know that your Mierda Moment has arrived. When that happens make the most out of it.

While you wait for the next Mierda Moment to hit you, reflect on if you have ever experienced it in the past. If so, what did it feel like, what was the effect? What came out of it?

One chapter soaked in anxiety. One chapter about the joy of being free from it. The creative life requires you to be able to embrace the pain of frustration as well as to have the wisdom to distance yourself from anxiety altogether.

Two seemingly contradictory messages one after the other. But that is the point: Do not let anyone tell you that there is just one approach to creativity.

Take an idea nap (Bangkok, Thailand)

One of the most refreshing insights I have ever gotten around the creative process came in the tiny studio of Kay, a Thai paper artist who creates stunning, intricate flowers and plants by cutting and folding paper. Her personality is just what you would imagine from a Thai origami artist: calm and serene and joyful and happy. She is the kind of person who seems genuinely grounded. Just sitting down and talking to her calmed my heart.

I met with her in her art studio located in a quiet corner of the otherwise bustling metropolis that is Bangkok to discuss her creative process. After a while our conversation wandered toward the theme of creator's block, i.e. the 'overwhelming feeling of being stuck in the creative process without the ability to move forward and make anything new'.

When I brought up the topic of creator's block with Kay she looked genuinely confused – as if she did not understand what I was talking about.

She smiled (she does that a lot) and said: 'Of course I (sometimes) get some stress from my work (but) I just keep saying to myself "Keep doing it, because creativity is a process. Keep doing it, even though you are tired". (And if you are tired, of course) take a rest. And then go back to the work again'.

She said it with such a carefree and worry-free expression that I had to ask again: 'So you do not worry when you get stuck?'

With her ever-reoccurring smile she explained: '(If I get stuck) I let (the creative project I am working on) rest for a while.

Just let it rest for a while. Refresh your thought. And then (go) back to it again'.

And then it struck me: This is a woman who has never suffered from creative anxiety.

I asked her to describe her process for when she gets stuck and she said: '(If I get stuck) I just go out of the studio and have some coffee or something. To clean my mind. To not be too stuck on that thing. It's kind of a reboot of the energy'.

When I asked her what was on her mind at that moment, she replied: 'What am I going to eat?'

I was confused.

So, nothing about the project? Not trying to solve the problem?

She (again) smiled, and said: 'No, not at all'.

Kay calls this approach of 'unanxiously' taking a break for 'Taking an idea nap'.

In her words: **'An idea nap is like a power nap for your creativity. (Sometimes) you have to take a rest and clean your head'.**

According to Kay, this way of thinking is deeply ingrained in the Thai mentality: '(In Thailand) we try to make it easy, we try to let it go. We have a Thai word called *sabai*, it's in the genes of the Thai people'.

According to Things Asian, 'the word *sabai* can be translated as "happy", but its use is often closer to "comfortable", "relaxed" or "well". To Thais, happiness is not a state opposite that of sorrow. Rather, it is more akin to tranquillity. Sitting by the seaside with the wind blowing in your hair is sabai. Winning the lottery is not. Thai offers many ways to intensify an adjective. One way is simply to repeat it. Thus, sabai sabai could be translated into English slang as "everything's chill" or "not a care in the world". It is wellness almost beyond words, the Thais' heaven on earth'.

If you have ever been to Thailand and, in a frustrated voice, asked the bartender when the beer you ordered 20 minutes ago is coming, you have probably been met with a friendly Thai smile, and a relaxed 'Sabai, sabai'. As in: 'Do not worry. Relax. Enjoy life. The beer will come'.

Sabai sabai is about not letting the problem define you. It is about knowing that whatever problem you are facing the solution will present itself soon so you might as well enjoy life while you wait for that moment. And this approach to life is not just making people happy, it is also perfect for the creative process – since creativity thrives when we are relaxed and worry free. The skill—because it is a skill—to take an idea nap, where you temporarily leave a creative project to do something else you enjoy, is a creative superpower.

When I leave Kay's office and walk out into the hot and humid Bangkok night, I feel lighter. **The insight that one can get stuck in a creative project without having to add anxiety or stress to one's life is liberating.**

Reflection

Learn from the Thais: Anxiety does not have to be part of the creative process.

Try this for a week: Every time you find yourself stuck in a creative project try leaving the project on your desk; stand up and say to yourself: 'Sabai, sabai. Time for an idea nap'. Then leave the project behind, take a break and try not to feel bad about it. After a well-deserved break – with as little anxiety as you can muster – go back to what you were working on and start creating again. The first few times it will probably feel weird, uncomfortable or useless, but keep doing it. Habits take time to form, and trust me, building a habit of being able to take a break from a creative project without feeling anxious or bad about it is a huge improvement in creative life quality.

An origami artist in Bangkok and an Afghan painter – two women with very different lives have two different lessons in creativity. Yes, there is always a connection. In this case the connection is about using time as your ally.

Profound Patience (Interview with an Afghan. Via Zoom)

For some people, there is a tendency to look at the creative process as something destructive. They will talk about things like 'radical disruption', 'revolutionary change', 'dramatic breakthroughs', etc. They are driven by the mantra of always be 'challenging the Status Quo'.

The same people tend to also look at creativity and innovation as something that is – or at least should be – fast. They will talk about the importance of being 'agile', of practising 'rapid prototyping' and will advocate for the need for 'accelerated change' and 'quick pivots'.

A typical example of this mindset is Facebook founder Mark Zuckerberg saying things like: 'Move fast and break things. Unless you are breaking stuff, you are not moving fast enough'.

I am not implying that Mark is wrong – speed and disruption have their place in creativity, and he has clearly been successful with that strategy of his – **but the wonderful thing with the creative process is that you can always find an alternative mindset that makes just as much sense.**

Introducing the concept of Profound Patience – a mindset toward creativity that is basically the total opposite of what Mark is talking about.

And, Sughra, the person who introduced me to the idea of Profound Patience, is also the total opposite of the white, male, tech-focused, billionaire American that is Mark Zuckerberg.

Sughra was born in Afghanistan. She lost her father when she was nine years old, and when she was fourteen, she also lost her mother. As a teenage girl, she found herself alone in a war-torn country, tasked with having to care for her younger siblings. A life so fundamentally different from that of Mr. Zuckerberg's that they are almost opposites.

To figure out a way to make a living to support herself and her siblings, Sughra started studying calligraphy and miniature painting at the Turquoise Mountain Institute.

Sughra, who, later in life, got a chance to escape the oppressive environment of her country and move to Washington, DC, told me about what studying traditional Afghan painting techniques had taught her about the creative process.

Looking at the ultra-conservative and highly restrictive regime of today's Afghanistan it might surprise some to learn that during the Timurid Empire (1370–1507), Afghanistan was a creative and cultural powerhouse. The golden age of Persian painting started during the Timurid Empire, and Sughra, who is a graduate of Turquoise Mountain Institute in Kabul, Afghanistan, has studied the calligraphy and painting techniques of that time.

When Sughra says that she creates her paintings from scratch, she is not kidding around. Before she can even begin to add the first paint stroke, she first must create her own paper, make her own paint and craft her own paintbrushes. That means that she will cut down wood to make pulp that she turns into paper. She will grind down precious stones into a fine powder that she turns into paint, and she will cut hair from the neck of a cat and tie it to a wooden stick to turn it into a brush. These tasks take weeks, if not months, to complete, which means that for a very long time before Sughra actually starts to put any paint on her canvas, she can only think about what she is going to paint. And this is where Profound Patience comes in. Sughra shared with me that the idea for a painting that she has in the beginning of the process is virtually never the idea for a painting that she starts to paint. By having to wait for weeks before she can paint, the initial idea transforms in her head.

Sughra: **'You have to give yourself time to improve on your idea. If you do not have patience, you cannot have good results. With patience I get more time to think creatively – it gives more opportunities for thinking better'.**

When Sughra arrived in the West, she was amazed – and a bit shocked – by how people in the West rushed creativity. In a world where you can get same-day-delivery of paper, paint and brushes so that you can start painting right after the urge to paint sets in, there is no space or time for reflection.

Or in the words of Sughra: 'If you always "hurry, hurry, hurry," you mess up everything'.

According to her, Profound Patience leads to patience and patience leads to yourself getting enough time to re-think your idea and make it better.

Just as good wine and good cheese will benefit from careful ageing in the right environment, so too will great ideas flourish if we give ourselves the luxury of taking our time with that which we create.

Sughra talks about 'giving yourself time to improve, because patience makes everything better'. We have to realise that the first idea that comes to our mind might not be the best one.

I asked Sughra how it feels when she, after weeks of preparations, finally gets to start to paint. Her eyes lit up and she said with a smile: 'It's a great, great feeling'.

When you've been grinding paint for weeks and making a brush from a cat's hair just to be able to paint, the reward of finally starting is immense.

Reflection

They say revenge is a dish best served cold, and there's some truth to that. But perhaps we should also consider creativity as a delicacy that benefits from a slow, patient ageing – allowing ideas to deepen, enrich and reach their full potential over time. Creativity, too, is a dish that, at least sometimes, benefits from being served cold.

Procrastination is often seen as a big enemy of creativity, and in many ways, it can be, but as we learned in this chapter, the creative process is littered with apparent contradictions, and sometimes it can be hugely beneficial to let the creative process take *more* time.

So let's practice 'deliberate procrastination'. Pick a creative project you are working on and give yourself a considerably longer deadline to finish it. I am talking about extending the deadline 10 times further into the future. If you normally plan your summer vacation a month in advance, try planning the one for the summer after next instead. But do not *decide* where to go now, instead journal your creative process and how your planning of your vacation changes when you have more than a year to execute it. Then go over your notes when the project is finally done and notice what you have done and how your ideas changed, transformed and developed when they were freed from the chains of urgency.

Profound patience teaches us to slow down and give our creativity time and space. Sometimes that is exactly what we need to do. And sometimes we need to do something very different: we need to challenge ourselves.

For our next chapter, we journey to New Zealand to do just that. Our teacher is a master at challenging his assumptions.

Find your challenger (Wellington, New Zealand)

A few years ago, on a hike through giant ferns in the forests on the outskirts of Wellington, I listened to Derek Sivers lay out his thoughts around what would become his book *How to live*. I had flown to meet with him because he is one of the most refreshingly creative minds I have ever had the privilege of meeting.

In his book *How to live*, each chapter makes the argument for how you should live your life. But each chapter disagrees with the next. Chapter 1, for example, is called 'Be independent' while Chapter 2 is called 'Commit'. And so on.

He argues strongly and succinctly for one extreme way to live one's life, and then, in the next chapter, argues for something completely different.

The book is a masterclass in the art of challenging oneself.

When I was young, my twin brother and I would pick a topic to discuss and then furiously argue two opposing views on that topic. After a while we would switch sides and continue the argument but now from totally opposite positions. It not only built rhetorical skills, but it also developed our creative skills. Try it sometime: Pick a position you firmly believe to be true. Then furiously argue against it.

Remember, creativity is not about finding 'the truth'.

But creativity is about being true – and the only way to do that is by being open to challenging everything. Even one's most fundamental beliefs.

This is a skill that can, and should, be practised.

(Derek is also a big fan of keeping writing short. So, in honour of him and his creativity, this chapter will be the shortest in this book and we end here.)

Reflection

Who in your life plays the role of making sure you challenge what you believe? Who is your challenger? How many people were you able to list? Could you benefit from having some more challengers?

Could you benefit from creating a structure that will challenge you in a more systematic and regular way?

Many entrepreneurs and other creatives have 'advisory boards', but perhaps we should have 'challenger boards'. Maybe you should have one? A challenger board could include someone with opposing values than you, someone who disagrees with your core assumptions or just someone with a very different worldview than yours. It could also be a good friend who you trust and respect, but who also has great integrity and the rhetorical skill of being able to really question your choices. Give your challenger board direct instructions to question your creative decisions in order to provoke new insights in you.

The fourth creative continent: Learning: The foundation of creative growth

Insights around how learning enhances creativity.

Sincerity in learning (Jakarta, Indonesia)

Interview enough really creative people and you will come to realise the one thing that keeps coming back over and over again: their love of learning. Yes, their love of learning how to become better, but it is more than that: It's the love of learning for the sake of learning. They do not approach creativity just as a way of creating. They approach creativity as a way to learn. Not just learning how to create but learning to understand the process.

If you want to become truly creative, you need to stop thinking about 'creating' and start applying a mindset of 'sincerity in learning'.

I learned about 'sincerity in learning' from Mondo Gascaro. Mondo is an Indonesian musician who has dedicated his life to music. He was a founding member of the influential Indonesian band Sore, and his solo debut album, 'RAJAKELANA', was listed in The Jakarta Post's Top 10 Albums of the Decade. For decades, he has been an influential player in the Indonesian creative scene, working as a musician, a singer-songwriter, a music director, a record producer and more, but when I ask him to tell me which of all these titles resonates the most with him, he replied. 'None. (When) I wake up, I see myself as a music enthusiast, as a music aficionado – as a student of music. That's how I see myself'.

A student of music.

With the crazy Jakarta traffic as our background music, I ask him to elaborate on what he means by that. So, he did: 'When you decide you are going to be a musician, I think you commit to learning music your whole life. I love music and I think music is endless, for me, it is an endless subject to learn'.

According to Mondo, having a learning mindset to creativity changes what you create: 'When you say, "Okay, I'm a musician. I'm gonna create music", you're going to create music. But the music you're gonna create is based on something you already know, or you think you already know. But when you say, "I'm a student of music, I'm going to study music my whole life", it means you keep the curiosity, you keep your passion, your sense of wonderment. When you learn something, I think there is more energy, because you do it with the sincerity of your whole being'.

Mondo calls creating with a learning mindset 'soulful creating' compared with creating without a learning mindset, which he calls 'automatic creating'. Or in Mondo's words: 'One is like an artist. The other is like a machine'.

Soulful creating comes from a place of humility toward wanting to understand the process. But it's not about 'mastering the process', it's about 'mastering learning the process'.

Hearing Mondo talk about the love of learning the process, I was reminded of when I once interviewed a man, Lukki Viebahn, who was studying to become a brewmaster at the Bavarian State Brewery Weihenstephan in Germany. Weihenstephan is the oldest brewery in the world. Beer has been brewed at that location for almost a thousand years. I met Lukki over a glass of beer while he was studying at the brewery school next to the old brewery. He told me: 'There are two types of students who apply here: those who love drinking beer, and those who love the process of making beer. After the first year, almost all from one of these categories have quit: Guess which one?'

I guessed: 'The people who love drinking beer?'

Lukki confirmed that my guess was correct. Students who wanted to become brewers simply because they loved beer often lost interest. They were overwhelmed by everything they had to learn about the brewing process. They did not love the process; they loved the result. But the people who love the process of beer making just love to learn more and more about that process itself. The beer is just the end result of that process. These brewers love learning through understanding the process of making the beer.

If you want to master a creative art, ask yourself which process you love, not what creative result you love.

According to Mondo, the trick to becoming truly creative is to approach any creative endeavour with this question in your mind: 'I am the student, who is my teacher?'

The teacher could be the process, it could be a person, it could be a mistake, it could be a lesson, it could be inspiration.

As Mondo said: 'I think the teacher could be everyone. And everything'.

If everything is a teacher, then nothing is a failure. Everything is a lesson.

If everyone is a teacher, then mentors are everywhere, and competition is nowhere.

If creating is an act of sincere learning, then creativity is about personal growth.

If creativity is about the love of learning the process, then the end result is not what matters.

Or as a creativity explorer might put it: 'Learning from the process is the journey. And the journey is the destination'.

Reflection

Mondo is a student of music. I am a student of, or more specifically, an explorer of, creativity. What are you a student of? I am not just talking about learning something while you create, I am talking about the fundamental thing you are here to study. With the answer to that core question in mind, how could you enhance the learning of that? For example, when I understood that exploring creativity meant I had to add a global perspective to my study of the topic, I grew profoundly. When I realised I needed to broaden my field of study outside the traditional creative fields, my world grew even more. From the perspective of being a student, how do you need to broaden your world?

And finally, a very practical question: For a creative project you are working on at the moment: If you are the student, then who – or what – is your teacher?

From an Indonesian musician telling us to be open to the idea of the many teachers – let's think of that as a horizontal learning approach to creativity. To a Bhutanese fashion designer elaborating about going deeper into the subprocesses – let's think of that as a vertical learning approach to creativity. Both sections apply humble curiosity toward learning more.

Creativity is so much about learning. For the first time in this book, let's trek to Bhutan.

Fractaling (Thimphu, Bhutan)

Sometimes, one sentence can open up your mind to an insight. That happened to me while sitting in a café in Thimphu as Bhutanese fashion designer Chandrika Tamang said to me: 'Every subprocess is an art'.

Chandrika Tamang is the founder of CDK Gyencha, a sustainable fashion brand that seamlessly blends traditional Bhutanese textiles with contemporary designs. With her statement of 'Every subprocess is an art' she invited me, over a cup of tea, into a conversation about going deeper into any creative work we are doing. What followed was a discussion about the beauty of going into the subprocesses of what we do. Something I have come to call 'Fractaling'.

In geometry, a fractal is 'a shape made up of parts that are the same shape as itself and are of smaller and smaller sizes'.

For creativity, 'fractaling' is the ability to see the beauty of a subprocess (and its subprocesses) in order to master what you are trying to create. To understand that any art is made up of sub-arts. The most creative people in any field will have understood this.

A great chef will not just master cooking but also will go and visit the farmer to learn more about how the produce she is using is grown. A great farmer, in turn, will visit the manufacturer of his farm equipment to better understand how to grow that same produce. And so on. Every art, every skill, is made up of other arts, of other skills. And the art (or the skill), if you will, is to understand this and embrace it.

Anyone who knows anything about making a movie will know that a great director will talk to the cinematographer to better understand the sub-art of filming and the cinematographer will talk to the people making her equipment to better understand how to master her own art. And so on.

A great guitarist will talk to the person who creates his guitar, who in turn will talk to the people who supply the wood for the instrument to better understand how to create the perfect guitar.

All the examples above are examples of 'creative fractaling' – becoming better at your own art by appreciating the beauty of the sub-arts that make up your own.

As a fashion designer, Chandrika's subprocesses are things like weaving, sewing, colouring, etc.

When I met with her, Chandrika was busy creating an exhibition about all the different subprocesses that can be found just in weaving, as a tribute to all the local Bhutanese weaving artists. In it, she was showcasing the art of spinning, the art of yarning, the art of looming, the art of weaving and so on.

And then, when the woven fabric is done, the fabric is taken to a seamstress and a whole new subprocess – the subprocess of sewing – begins.

When I bring up sewing in our conversation, her eyes light up and she bursts out, full of energy: 'Yes. Sewing is a huge art in itself. It has so many segments'.

On the surface, it looks like a fashion designer like Chandrika designs a garment, but the finished piece is just the tip of the iceberg. That jacket we see on the runway is actually the result of almost infinite subprocesses, and the better a designer understands each one, the more creative opportunities open up.

Going down the path of 'creative fractaling' triggers a deeper understanding of our own subject, ignites curiosity and broadens our creativity.

We can always go deeper.

So go deeper.

Reflection

Map out your own creative fractal structure. What are all the subprocesses of your creative expression of choice? What are all the subprocesses of those subprocesses? Build a family tree of subprocesses as far as you can go. Then go to your favourite search or AI tool and ask it to teach you something about each subprocess that someone higher up in the process should know.

Which of all these subprocesses intrigues or inspires you the most to want to learn more about it? Use the curiosity generated by this to dig deeper into that specific subprocess.

We linger in Bhutan for a second section.

The main themes of each section are different:
one is about going deeper into your
subprocesses, one is about thinking differently
about how we interact with the creativity
of others.

One teacher is a fashion designer.
One is a government official.

The common thread is the value of conscious,
active participation for creativity.

(And yes, this contradicts other sections in this
book, which push the idea that creativity is
best nurtured by the subconscious mind.)

Evoking creativity (Thimphu, Bhutan)

When it comes to creativity, there is, amongst many, a view of 'first class' and 'second class'. First class are the people who create. Second class are the people who 'consume' creative content.

Writing a book is much 'better' than reading the same book.

Performing a piece of music is much 'better' than listening to it being played.

And of course, enjoying a creative work is not, at all, the same creative act as creating it, but 'consuming' creative work has gotten an undeserved bad reputation. **Just the fact that we call it 'consuming', which indicates 'to devour, to destroy, as by decomposition or burning' indicates that we tend to look at being on the receiving end of creativity as something negative.**

A fire consumes a forest. And a reader consumes a book.

But musicians know that to become great musicians they need to listen to music.

Painters know that to become great painters they need to enjoy art.

And writers know that to be good writers they need to read.

Or to quote Stephen King in his epic book *On writing*: 'Reading is the creative centre of a writer's life'.

Thinking of users of creative work as simply 'consumers' of it reduces the act of enjoying creative work. It implies passivity and destruction. It suggests we are just 'using up' something, rather than engaging with it. 'Consuming' does not reflect the emotional transformation, or the bursts of inspiration and growth that enjoying someone else's creative work can trigger.

We should stop thinking of ourselves as merely consumers of creativity and begin to appreciate the art of receiving creative work as the strong emotional activity that it is. Because creativity evokes so much in us.

The person who got me thinking of creativity in terms of evoking was Sonam Penjor. He is the director of the Department of Media, Creative Industry & Intellectual Property for the government of Bhutan and I met with him in his sparsely decorated office in the capital of Thimphu.

Sonam is not your average government official. He has a creative soul to complement an administrative mind. And he has a huge smile and an even bigger heart. He is the kind of public servant who will go down to the local rap scene in Thimphu and invite the kids to perform an Eminem song, only to join them in the performance because he knows the lyrics. He is passionate about the power of creativity.

Listening to Sonam describe his love for enjoying the creative work of others gave me a deeper appreciation for being on the receiving end of creativity.

Sonam told me: 'When I listen to a song, or watch a movie, (or any other creative content) I do that with a purpose. I want to evoke an emotion in me. For example, in the morning I might want to listen to some very peppy music because I want to awaken myself. I want to rise. I want to shine. When I use someone else's creative work I want that work to evoke an emotion in me. When we utilize their creation, we should emote some emotion in ourselves. Consuming someone else's creative work is a conscious act to evoke an emotion'.

Listening to Sonam I realised that creativity is not just 'consumed'. It is 'evoked'.

Evoking Creativity is about using the creative work of others to trigger emotional reactions in oneself. Evoking Creativity is a conscious act.

Consuming is passive.
Evoking is active.

Consuming is destructive.
Evoking is generative.

Consuming is depleting
Evoking is replenishing.

Of course, sometimes we just want to consume some creative work, like when we want to be entertained, distracted or just want to kill some time. And that is fine.

But other times we want to be inspired, awakened, emotionally charged. Evoked.

This kind of creative absorption is so different from merely 'consuming' creativity that the term 'evoking creativity' is needed to differentiate the two ways of being on the receiving end of creativity.

Sonam approaches creativity wholeheartedly. He doesn't just put on 'some music', he deliberately picks the artist he wants to listen to, researches them, reads the lyrics and listens actively.

Creative people do this. They see other creative people's work as a source of inspiration. As a teacher. As energy.

I asked Sonam for some advice on how to let creativity evoke emotions and he replied:

'It's a very difficult question. But from my experience: Be in the moment. When you are receiving creative work, be in the moment. Be there. Be there'.

Reflection

The next few times when you are going to enjoy the creative work of others, do not just 'consume it'. Instead, practise intentional evoking. Be intentional with both the creative work you select and how you choose to enjoy it, as well as what emotions or reactions you hope to trigger.

For example, do not just 'put on some music', but ask your AI assistant to recommend a song to inspire risk-taking.

Done right the creative work of others can fuel you in so many different ways. But only if you make a decision to let it. So decide to let it.

If the last section was about letting in the creativity of others, the next is about rethinking how we let our own creativity flow back into our lives to inspire us. Let's listen to an Australian about creative inlets.

Look for creative inlets – Not just creative outlets (Melbourne, Australia)

Many people look for a hobby outside their work as a creative outlet for their souls. The idea is good, creativity should always be encouraged, but the approach is not the best. **Even better than a creative outlet is a creative inlet.** Let me explain.

I learned about creative inlets from Georgina Yen Qin Lee. Georgina was previously the Innovation, Growth and Experience Leader at Mercer Australia. Mercer is a global consulting firm, and Georgina loved her job. But that was not always the case.

As a creative and artist at heart, for many years, her job at Mercer was merely a way to make a living to support her art practice. But it was not where she got her creative inspiration. Georgina would get her 'creative fix' working as an artist in the evenings, working with start-ups on design strategy or being involved with independent arts organisations.

The job at Mercer was well paid, but in many situations, corporate life was 'killing her soul'. All the creative side hustles were what kept her soul alive.

Many people believe their day job cannot fulfil their creative potential. This creates a widespread notion that creativity requires side activities, hobbies or pro-bono work. Serious at work. Creative during our free time.

But while we might have different identities, we are just one person. Separating our 'creative selves' from our 'professional selves' could risk making us miserable, or at least much less creative than we could be.

Georgina is a person who loves being creative. All the time. She looks nothing like what you would expect from a person in a corporate environment with her coloured hair and plentiful tattoos. And she told me about how her hunger for creativity outside of work 'infected' her working style at work.

She took the creative energy that was generated during her 'off work' creative projects and used it to bring an element of creativity into her projects at the office. And people noticed. Slowly, she got more and more creative assignments to work on. One day, she saw herself being recruited as chief of staff to the Mercer Australia CEO and one of the reasons the CEO wanted to work with her specifically was, according to the CEO, her ability to think in creative ways.

Finally, she ended up landing a role as Innovation, Growth and Experience Leader in a big part because of her ability to bring the creative energy from her side hustles into her day job. As Georgina put it: 'You are exercising your brain in different ways. Bring that mindset into your daily work and you will find that you will gravitate to more creative projects at work. And eventually, that work will start gravitating to you'.

The creative projects that she had looked at as 'outlets' were actually 'inlets'.

An 'outlet' is 'a pipe or hole through which water or gas may escape'. Why look at creative energy as something that is escaping?

An 'inlet' is 'a place or means of entry'. So, look at creative side projects as places or means of entry for your creative energy and that energy can then be transferred to the rest of your life.

Georgina has since left the corporate world completely after finding success in her ceramics business, Yen Qin. Now working full-time as an artist and designer, she draws on her years of strategic and commercial experience – again, not as a contrast to creativity, but as an inlet into it. Her business blends cultural storytelling with design-led tableware, shaped as much by intuition as by intention. It's a shift from board-rooms to the potter's wheel, but one that still centres on shaping ideas into form and building something that lasts.

Follow the lead of Georgina, who not only practised this idea of finding creative energy outside of work on herself but who also encourages others to find creative projects outside work that will create positive creative energy that they can harness at work. Because Georgina has discovered the creative power that resides in having 'creative inlets'.

And so should the rest of us.

Reflection

Do a creative energy audit to identify where your creative energy flows. List your creative outlets (energy flowing out) and your creative inlets (energy flowing in). Identify your strongest creative inlets and consider how you could broaden them even more. Also, reflect on whether there is any additional creative inlet that you need to create to open up for more positive creative energy to flow into you.

From leveraging the creative system of inlets to leveraging the creative system of thinking in patterns. One inspired by a ceramics artist, one inspired by a YouTuber. Creatives really come in all shapes and forms, and they are all over the world.

We leave Melbourne and Georgina and visit piano virtuoso Ray Mak in Kuala Lumpur next.

Thinking in patterns to think faster
(Kuala Lumpur, Malaysia)

Contrary to popular belief, repetition is not the enemy of creativity but its foundation, because it trains the mind to perceive structures that can later be creatively reassembled into something new.

This is crucial for creativity, because by learning something by repetition, we learn how to see and recognise patterns, and when we can see and recognise patterns, we can think on a different scale.

In its rawest of forms, an idea is just a combination of already known things, as described in the chapter about China and 'copying right'. By learning to see patterns, we get the ability to combine larger entities. Instead of seeing small things that we can combine, we can combine big things together.

Consider this analogy: instead of seeing individual planets, we can learn to recognise larger patterns. We combine planets into solar systems, then solar systems into galaxies. Each level reveals bigger patterns we can work with. And then, suddenly, we can combine a galaxy with another galaxy, and we create on a totally different level than just seeing planet by planet.

The better we become at seeing patterns, the bigger our ability to combine things on a larger scale.

Thinking in patterns makes us faster thinkers. And bigger thinkers.

One of my first jobs was to work as a croupier in a casino. Non-croupiers would be amazed by how quickly we could calculate the winnings on roulette, but a croupier does not add every single marker one by one; instead, they see patterns of combinations of chips that they then can combine into the correct amount to be paid.

All creative people have an enhanced ability to think in larger patterns.

One person who helped me show the advantage of thinking in patterns was Ray Mak. Ray is a musician with an impressive ability to play any song on his piano after just hearing it once, or twice. His skills as a piano player have given him over 100,000,000 views on YouTube and a channel with almost 500,000 followers. He was one of the first YouTubers in Malaysia to make it big.

I met with Ray in his home studio to talk about how pattern recognition helps him create faster.

Sitting at his piano, he told me: 'Repetition is the mother of all skills, so that's just what I believe. I wasn't born with this, like savant syndrome kind of thing of being able to copy music, it's just that I repeat it so often that I'm able to pick it faster, and faster, and faster'.

Having practised for years, Ray can quickly pick up patterns in any song, which makes it easier for him to pick up the notes vs trying to pick up and remember each individual note.

This skill, let's call it HLC (as in 'high-level creativity'), is the ability to combine patterns instead of individual items. It is what makes it possible for someone to create on a higher level.

Ray: 'To be creative, you have to have the ability to think in patterns'.

So, think in patterns, see patterns, recognise patterns, train yourself to understand patterns and you will become even more creative.

Reflection

It's time to spend some time recognising our pattern recognition skills. In Ray's case, he uses pattern recognition to help identify music quickly. In your case, what pattern recognition do *you* use to speed up your creative work? We all use patterns, but most people are not aware of how instrumental pattern recognition is for the skills they master. Identifying these patterns could help make your creative process even faster. And here is a 'meta exercise' you can do: once you have identified what patterns you rely on for your creative process, sit down with a piece of paper (or input the list into your favourite AI tool) and try to extract a pattern around the patterns that you just described. A pattern, after all, is a recognisable arrangement of elements, but to fully take advantage of the shortcut that pattern recognition is we need to be aware of the patterns that we are using.

The fifth creative continent: Collaborating and communicating for creativity

Thoughts on how to share, develop and realise ideas with others.

The 'Videmus' moment (Bucharest, Romania)

That exact moment when we have an idea is arguably the most well-described aspect of the creative process. It has been given many names: The 'A-ha' moment. The 'Lightbulb' moment. The 'Eureka' moment.

Most of us are familiar with the story of Archimedes in his bathtub, bursting out, 'I have found (it)!' (*Heureka* in Greek), when he solved the problem of telling whether King Hiero II's crown was made of pure gold or whether it was just gold-plated. That second when we have a really good idea is an amazing moment. There is a reason why the words 'creativity' and 'creator' (as in God) have the same root. You could even argue that we never feel closer to God (or to being gods) than when we have a really good idea. Time stands still. Angels sing. We feel at one with the universe and we see the light. No wonder Archimedes is said to have run around naked on the streets of Syracuse screaming with joy after his 'Eureka' moment.

But I am going to argue that there is an even more magical moment in the creative process than having a great idea: I am talking about the first time another person understands the greatness of your idea. I call it the Videmus moment. It's Latin for 'We see' – as in the first time a person says 'Oh, I see!', and you finally feel that you are not alone with your idea anymore. You have found someone to share your joy with. You are no longer the only person who sees the potential of the idea. **And just like love, laughter and good memories, ideas become better when you have someone to share them with.**

I learnt about the Videmus moment from Andi Daiszler from the Daisler Association in Romania. Andi runs a flower festival that happens once a year (in June, in Cluj-Napoca). It brings more than 10,000 people to a short, narrow street in his city. The street, called Potaissa (which also gave the event its name), was unloved by the people and city planners of Cluj until Andi had the idea to turn it into the most beautiful street in the city once a year by dressing it up in flowers, inviting musicians to play and restaurants to set up tables where cars would normally be parked.

In the beginning, it was very hard to get people excited about how this street, that no one cared about, had the potential to become a place of beauty and joy. But Andi persisted, and he vividly remembers exactly when he had the Videmus moment. It was the first year of the festival and they had put up a light sign above the street that said Mi-e Dor De Tine, i.e. 'I miss you'. The sign was there to send the message that when the festival would be over in a few days, and the street went back to being a normal, dull and boring backstreet of the city, the people would miss what had been created there. On the first day of the festival in year one, Andi saw a taxi driver who stopped his car, smiled a broad smile and took a picture of the street, the flowers and the light sign. He then sent the photo to someone else. A taxi driver taking a photo of his flowers and light sign – Andi knew the idea had broken through to the rest of the world.

Together with Andi Daiszler we came up with the word 'idealing' to describe the process. **Idealing is a combination of 'idea' and 'seedling'. When we have an idea, we see its potential, but no one else does. You know the potential of a seed that is in the ground. But when the seed breaks out of the ground and others can see it too, its potential spreads to others.** The seed has become a seedling. The moment when your idea becomes an idealing is the Videmus moment.

Sometimes the moment never comes. A person has, what they think is, a wonderful idea, but no matter how many times the idea is shared with others, or how well it is described or pitched, no other human being sees the potential of the idea. That could, of course, be because the idea is actually not very good. But the history of the world is, unfortunately, filled with great ideas that their creators took to their graves without anyone else ever recognising their greatness. **When you think about how those ideas could have made the world better, had someone just seen their brilliance, you realise that this might very well be one of the saddest things we humans do to each other.**

Luckily, our world is also full of those wonderful moments when a creative person was able to show/convince/communicate to others what a great idea they have had.

The Videmus moment is not necessarily the first time you share your idea with someone else. Sometimes you describe your idea to many people, and no one gets even remotely as excited as you about the potential of your ideas. Then suddenly you present the idea to a person and their eyes light up, they smile that silly-yet-intelligent smile of epiphany. Angels sing. They have seen the potential of your idea, and you can see that they have. And you feel great.

J.K. Rowling had to send her manuscript to 12 publishers before Bryony Evans at Christopher Little Literary Agency fell in love with Harry, Hermione and all the other characters of Hogwarts. That moment, when Rowling got a call from Bryony

Evans from Christopher Little, and Evans shared how she loved Harry and the book and wanted to publish it, is a perfect example of the Videmus moment. She saw something that 12 other publishers had not seen, but that Rowling had been living with for 7 years since the idea of Harry Potter came to her in a 'Eureka' moment on a train between Manchester and London.

Andi Daiszler from the Daisler Association also told me about another memorable Videmus moment. He and some friends created a light art festival called 'Lights On Romania'. One of the artworks they brought in was a huge, inflatable balloon resembling the Moon, which they placed inside a Catholic church, the Piarist Church in Cluj, Romania. At first, people were sceptical ('A moon in a church?'). But then they invited Romanian schoolchildren from working-class families to the church. The kids came from villages and had very little exposure to art. Andi described how the children would simply freeze at the entrance to the church when they saw the huge art installation. Other children behind them would bump into those in front. The intense emotional reaction to experiencing art on this scale for the first time blew their minds. Andi Daiszler got confirmation that bringing a big light artwork in the likeness of the moon into a church was a good idea. It was a beautiful Videmus moment.

Treasure your 'Eureka' moments. Without them, we have no ideas. But also treasure those Videmus moments. **Someday, when you look back at your life, those moments when someone else, for the first time, saw the pure beauty of your best ideas will likely count among the best moments of your life.**

Reflection

Reflect on what has been the most powerful Videmus moment in your own life. It could be the first time someone 'got' one of your best ideas. But it could also be a 'pretty good' idea that no one believed in until suddenly, after hundreds of rejections, someone actually saw its potential.

Now, here is an important observation: Videmus moments can be *created*. By making it easier for people to see the brilliance of your idea, you, in the end, make it easier for your idea to become a reality. A powerful tool for creating Videmus moments is rhetoric. Very often, when people do not understand why an idea is brilliant, it is not because the idea is bad, it's because the idea is not presented well. Now, don't get me wrong: it *could* also be because the idea is bad ... but too many ideas have died on the hill of ignorance, because people who should have cared never understood. **Study rhetoric; it is the art of getting people to fall in love with your idea.**

Here is a very simple rhetorical rule you can use to get started: It is called The 4Ps. It stands for Position, Problem, Possibilities and Proposal.

Step 1. Do not start by describing the problem that your solution solves. Instead, start by describing a common reality that people will recognise. This is called 'The Position'. First, get people to agree on where we are.

Step 2. Next, state the problem. Get people to see what is wrong with the current situation.

Step 3. Paint a better world. Let people see the Possibilities of how things could improve.

Step 4. Propose your solution.

For illustrative purposes, I asked ChatGPT to give me a sample of how to use the 4Ps for trying to sell the idea of creating a flower festival in a local town:

Position (The current situation):

> 'Our town has beautiful gardens, talented florists, and nature lovers, but these talents are mostly enjoyed in small, scattered ways'.

Problem (What's wrong with this situation):

> 'We're missing an opportunity to bring the whole community together, attract visitors, and celebrate the beauty that's already around us'.

Possibilities (What could be better):

> 'Imagine a vibrant flower festival – with stunning displays, workshops, parades, and markets – that not only showcases local talent but also boosts tourism, supports local businesses, and creates lasting memories'.

Proposal (What to do):

> 'Let's launch an annual Flower Festival, starting small this year with a weekend event, building partnerships with local gardeners, businesses, and artists, and growing it year by year into a signature celebration for our town'.

Use the 4Ps, or any other rhetorical technique, to make it easier for people to fall in love with your idea.

While the Videmus moment might be beautiful when it arrives, we first have to understand that often, people might need some help or guidance to understand why the idea you are presenting to them is great. That is where Unalienising comes in.

Off to Ireland we fly to learn about Unalienising from a sausage maker.

Unalienising (Dublin, Ireland)

Have you ever faced resistance when introducing a new idea or innovation? Often, this pushback occurs because the novelty is perceived as alien. This is where the concept of 'unalienising' comes in.

The fact is that people trying to introduce new ideas, new innovations or new technology are often met with resistance because the novelty is seen as alien by other people.

By that, it follows that to get people to accept your idea, you need to unalienise it for them.

The art of unalienising can be defined as:

> *'The art of unalienising involves making something less alien or foreign by fostering familiarity, relatability, and inclusion. It's about transforming estrangement into a sense of belonging and connection'.*

I learned about the skill of unalienising during a conversation with Ashley Moran, Marketing and Category Director at Pilgrim's Food Masters in Ireland. Pilgrim's Food Masters is the United Kingdom's largest producer of delicious meats, chilled and frozen ready meals for every major UK and Ireland supermarket.

Ashley was part of the team that took meat-free sausages to market. She explained to me how the idea of launching a meat-free sausage was alien to most people within Pilgrim's Food Masters before the launch. Most people saw meat as the centre of what Pilgrim's Food Masters did. Ashley herself was, in the beginning, reluctant to see how successful a sausage with no meat could become.

But then she described the way she unalienised the idea of a plant-based sausage to herself. First, she went to trade fairs to try out what was on the market; then she visited the test kitchen where their own products were being developed and then she attended customer taste test events where she could study the reaction of potential customers.

She told me: 'In the beginning, I said to myself. "I just can't see this (plant-based sausages) taking off", but the more I studied it, the more I researched it, and – crucially – the more I tasted it, I slowly warmed to the idea'.

Ashley specifically remembers the day she was won over. She had just tried a plant-based sausage in which she really could not tell if it had meat or not. Suddenly, the idea of Pilgrim's Food Masters selling sausages with no meat was not alien to her anymore.

She calls this moment 'The Moment of Proof'. The Moment of Proof is the other side of the coin of 'The moment of truth'. The Moment of Truth is from the perspective of the person trying to get their idea accepted (in this case, the person *serving* the meat-free sausage). The Moment of Proof is from the perspective of the person there to be convinced. (In this case, Ashley being convinced that the meat-free sausage will work.)

The Moment of Proof is the moment when you feel that you have received enough proof/evidence/affirmation about something new that is presented to you that you are willing to buy into it.

I asked Ashley for three steps to become better at unalienising someone. She summed it up as follows:

(1) Seeing is believing.
Get people to experience it.

Ashley: 'Having us develop our first meat-free sausage was so important for us to warm to the idea'.

(2) Reassurance is reassuring.
To get people open to new ideas they need to feel that things are going in the right direction, so search for situations where that positive momentum can be experienced.

Ashley: 'The lovely moment when you see the consumer liking (the meat-free sausage) gave us the confidence to move forward'.

(3) Engage to get engagement.
Create momentum by engaging the different stakeholders in making the idea happen.

Ashley: 'Engaging the business to get ready was crucial. That included getting our trade partners onboard to put the products on the shelf. We all got onboard'.

Finally, Ashley stresses the need for a safe environment when trying to unalienise someone to a new idea. Ashley: 'You need to be in a safe space that takes you in a good head space when trying to warm to a new idea'.

Hearing Ashley talk about the concept of unalienation, I get a picture of the movie E.T. in my head. **Just like Elliott in the movie E.T., who went from fear to friendship with the alien, unalienising involves a gradual process of acceptance and understanding.**

Reflection

**Unalienising is a process. That means you can struc-
ture it.** The next time you are getting ready to introduce
an idea to the world, create an 'unalienising plan' to help
your idea be accepted and adopted.

It can include answering questions such as:

What about your idea is alien to your intended audience?
How could you let them try it out in a safe way?
What can you do to get them on board?
What would make it feel less strange?

Unalienising is crucial for getting people to come around to your idea, but don't try too hard – stay true to your idea. Creativity Choreography, on the other hand, is about understanding that how someone receives your idea is beyond your control. We need both. First, create from an authentic self, then help others see what you imagined.

Creativity Choreography
(Copenhagen, Denmark)

'Choreography is composing movement'. The words belong to Lotte Sigh, a Danish choreographer, artistic director and teacher. Along with her freelance work, she is affiliated with The Royal Danish Ballet as a choreographer, teacher and examiner, and she also co-founded Copenhagen Contemporary Dance School. The Ballet is hosted in an old, beautiful building and the dance education is hosted in an old fire station. I met with her in the café of The National Library of Copenhagen, which is located between the two institutions. She has worked with dance her whole life, including in Holland, Italy, Spain, Switzerland and the United States, with choreographic practice as the core of her work.

I met with her because I wanted to understand what we can learn about the creative act of creating something others are to perform. It turned out to be a conversation about how to think about creativity in general.

Dance is a powerful medium of expression. A language of the body. A language to the soul.

It can trigger such powerful emotions and reactions. Dance is an energy like no other.

To illustrate the power of dance, Lotte told me about a project she was working on with Copenhagen International Dance Festival: '(In this project) we take dancing to different care institutions. We go out to people who are stuck in a bed or to hospital equipment. When we go there, I can just see that the movement always – with no exception – brings energy. I remember how we went to one of these places to dance and in the audience was Karen who was 92 years old. She had dementia and had been sitting with her head on the table for six months. And once the dancers started to move, she woke up. The staff was in tears because they were so happy to see Karen come to life again. **Dance does that. Dance brings a feeling of energy, a feeling of inspiration and hope. And an openness. It also brings love, care and community'.**

Yes, dance is a powerful way of communicating. And a choreographer is the person responsible for envisioning and shaping the physical poetry of the body. The word 'Choreography' literally means 'to write down dance', but Lotte was quick to explain that while she writes down how the dancers should move, she is not telling them how to receive her instructions or what to do with them on a deeper level.

Because she cannot.

No one can.

It's impossible to tell someone else how to react or how to receive a message. However, the dancers' reactions are essential for the final poetry, since choreography is so much more than movement in time and space.

Lotte: 'I have a vision, and bringing it to life takes trust and communication between me and the dancers. In that way, choreography is unique. I cannot do this alone, and that is the beauty of it. To put it a little bluntly,I have never worked on anything where I wanted the audience to feel or think a specific thing. (When I worked) on the choreography, I had a clear idea of what I wanted to communicate, but how the dancers, or the audience, receive it, I would never try to dictate that at all'.

Lotte likens the transfer of a creative work to throwing a metaphorical ball to someone (a dancer, or an audience) and then the other party does with it what they want. What that is, is out of your control. And that is how it should be. She said: 'I hope they react and throw the ball back. Action and reaction are the essence of human   communication and the most interesting part of it all'.

So, what should one do in the creative process? Lotte's answer can be summarised as: 'Focus on your action, not their reaction (when it comes to the audience)'.

The reactions matter; that's why I create. But in the creative process, I focus on what I wish to contribute. If you try to "put yourself in the heads of others" then you, by default, will be unauthentic, since that is impossible to do.

You can never control how someone reacts to something you have created.

So, stop trying to do that.

Instead, pour all your energy into what you can control: The work you are creating.

Do not write the song you think people want to hear. Write the song that is in you.

Do not write the LinkedIn post you think people want to read. Write the LinkedIn post you want to share.

Do not write a book you think someone wants. Write the book you must write.

And so on.

To be authentically creative is to bring out the message that is within you and to bring that out to the world to the best of your abilities. Creativity Choreography is about understanding that how someone receives your idea is beyond your control, and maybe also beyond your understanding. So do the best you can to manifest the idea that is within you, and that needs to get out. And focus on that. Not on how others might receive, perceive, interpret or judge what you have created.

Not only will the creative process become more enjoyable if you do that, but the end result will also be clearer and more genuine. **It will give freedom, to you and to the receiver.**

Reflection

Let's take a creative project that you are working on at the moment and work with that.

First, write a description of what you are creating, tailored to your intended audience.

Second, write a description of what you are creating based on why you are creating it.

Third, compare the two texts and reflect on the difference.

Fourth, embrace the second description and see how focusing on that helps you develop a more authentic idea.

For example, if I were to do this exercise for this book that you are reading, the first description would read:

'A book to help others understand creativity better'.

The second description would read:

'Get clarity on what creativity really is'.

And my analysis is: 'Don't try to teach—try to understand'.

That might not mean much to you, but it made me rewrite a large part of this book to change the tone I was using.

From insights from a contemporary choreographer in Denmark to lessons in how to effectively use inspiration as a tool from a hotel manager in the Maldives.

Two very different sections – united by a common theme: being intentional and active in the creative process.

Respiration – Turning inspiration into creative action (LUX South Ari Atoll, the Maldives)

At the LUX Resort in the Maldives, a floating sign reading **'Celebrate Life'** rises from the turquoise waters, creating a picture-perfect moment designed to inspire guests to capture and share it.

It works. When I was there, I took a boatload of selfies of me and my family with the happy message in the background, and my children still talk about that sign long after we were there.

There are countless beachside bars with stunning views around the world, but by adding that sign in the water, LUX South Ari Atoll created a small piece of extra value for their guests.

The Senior Director of Talent and Culture at LUX South Ari Atoll is Hussain Afeef, and while the idea of putting up that sign was not his, he is very much the person behind creating the culture at LUX resort that makes the people who work there constantly come up with ideas on how to make the resort even better.

Afeef is one of the most passionate lifelong learners I've encountered. Whether he's reading management books, attending conferences or working with mentors, he embodies the spirit of relentless self-improvement. It's not always the case to have an HR professional who is genuinely passionate about their own personal development – but with Afeef, it absolutely is.

Afeef lives and works on a tiny atoll that you reach by seaplane from Male, the capital of the Maldives. The Maldives is one of the most remote countries in the world. The country's closest neighbour, India, is 600 kilometres away, and virtually all things they need to survive, from oil to toilet paper, are shipped in by air or sea.

Afeef might live in a remote part of the world, but he refuses to be isolated. **To Afeef, isolation isn't a location – it's a mindset.**

Hussain Afeef has decided not to be isolated. He is extremely driven by the need to be inspired.

When I had the chance to sit down and learn from him, he started our conversation by saying: 'You have to make an effort to become creative'. This is a person who constantly and consistently improves himself.

The reason I sat down with him was because I wanted to understand how Afeef works with helping the staff at LUX Maldives become even more creative. What I learnt changed how I look at inspiration and its role in creativity.

We all know that inspiration plays a huge role in creativity, but Afeef gave me insights into the necessary bridge between inspiration and creativity. Let's call that bridge 'Creative Respiration'.

To understand the concept of 'Creative Respiration', we need to have a quick biology lesson. In creativity, inspiration is 'the process of being mentally stimulated to do or feel something, especially to do something creative', but the original meaning of the word is connected to how we breathe. Inspiration is 'the drawing in of breath; inhalation' from *spirare* meaning 'to breathe'.

However, just because we breathe in something does not mean that we will get any effect. For that, we need respiration. Respiration is 'a process in living organisms involving the production of energy, typically with the intake of oxygen'.

In biology, inspiration brings oxygen into the lungs, but respiration is the *transformation* of that oxygen into energy.

For creativity, we can think about it like this: Inspiration (in the meaning 'being mentally stimulated to do or feel something') is the oxygen to our creativity.

But for inspiration to *become* creativity, it needs to be transformed into energy. Or in other words, we need 'Creative Respiration'.

In Afeef's case, he sees it as one of his roles to not just share inspiring ideas with his staff, but to make sure that these ideas are transformed into creative energy.

He told me how he had been visiting Los Angeles on a research trip and found a new type of drink in one of the bars there. He took a picture of the drink and sent it to his bartender back on the island. When he was back at the resort, Afeef also made sure to visit the bartender to see if the photo he had sent had inspired some ideas. Together, they then tried to recreate the drink from Los Angeles.

Afeef went out of his way to make sure the inspiration he saw in Los Angeles turned into creative energy in the bartender.

I asked Afeef for the practical things we can do to make sure that inspiration is turned into respiration. Three things we can do to make sure inspiration is turned into creative energy. He said:

(1) **'Inspiration is an effort. Make it as effortless as possible to be inspired'.**

Most people have too many things going on with their normal workload, so when new things are sent to them with the intent of inspiring them, it might actually just make them stressed, distracted or overwhelmed. By making an effort to make sure that the inspiration he sends their way is delivered in a way that is easy to understand and simple to turn into action Afeef is making it easier for his staff to digest the new insights he is sending them.

(2) 'Celebrate the effort, not the result'.

If inspiration is going to contribute to creative output, we cannot let failure get in the way.

Once Afeef had shown his staff how other resorts invited famous chefs as guests to their restaurants which inspired the crew to create a 'Master Chef project' with invited celebrity chefs, but the concept did not fly, and the resort guests did not really appreciate the idea. But by celebrating the idea, the staff were motivated to tweak the concept and instead successfully launched a new service – inspired by the first try – where guests could cook with a local female chef. The concept was called 'Cook with a mother' and it is a huge success with the guests.

(3) 'Appreciate all ideas, but do not implement all ideas'.

All ideas generated from inspiration should be celebrated. That's how you keep the creative energy high. But just because you appreciate all ideas does not mean you should implement all ideas. There will always be more ideas out there than what we can implement, and not all ideas deserve to be implemented.

If a person sitting on the tiny island of Dhidhoofinolhu in the middle of the Arabian Sea can use the world as inspiration, then so can you. And inspired by the vast curiosity of Hussain Afeef you should also be inspired to, just like him, make sure that your inspiration is put into good use. Here's to you dedicating yourself to Creative Respiration.

Reflection

The author Jack London said, 'You can't wait for inspiration. You have to go after it with a club'. He is on to something, but inspiration is not enough; we also need to turn it into creative energy.

Make sure you are not just inspired by inspiration; make sure the inspiration is turned into creative respiration.

Write down 10 things that inspire you. Then write down *why* they inspire you. And in the next column, write down how that inspiration is turning into actual creative energy.

The third column is the most important one. **If you're inspired but it's not turning into creative work, you're experiencing what Afeef would call 'inspiration without respiration' – you're breathing in the creative oxygen but not converting it to energy.**

In your list, underline your answers that give you the most creative respiration. Reflect on how you can expose yourself to more inspiration that generates that effect in you.

The sixth creative continent: Mastery and transcendence

Advanced creative states and the deeper purposes of creativity.

Creativity is understanding yourself
(Paro, Bhutan)

The approach to Paro airport is one of the most beautiful approaches to any airport on Earth. The aeroplanes zig-zag between the mountain peaks until they land in the valley. There is something very unique about sitting in an aeroplane and looking up at a temple as you fly in to land.

Bhutan, the tiny Kingdom nestled into the mountains of the Himalayas, is unique in many ways, including how it has challenged how a country should measure success.

When the concept of 'Gross National Happiness' (GNH) was introduced to the world by the fourth King of Bhutan, Jigme Singye Wangchuck, it sent shockwaves through many governments around the world.

While virtually all other countries at the time had economic growth of a country – its GDP – as the main measurement stick, here was a country that had decided to put the happiness of its people at the centre.

It was such a fresh and different way of thinking about the purpose of government – and of what should, and should not, be measured.

And while some criticism has emerged around Bhutan's focus on Gross National Happiness, I think it's fair to say that the spirit of the idea is still groundbreaking, innovative and thought-provoking. Over the years, GNH has evolved, and it is now an established concept that influences how many governments and politicians think about their roles.

And now Bhutan is once again ready to shake up how we think about a concept. And this time, the concept is creativity.

The person who gave me a profoundly different perspective on creativity was Dorji Dhradhul, former Director General at the Royal Government of Bhutan (Tourism Council). Dorji has 32 years of service as a civil servant, including a stint as Dzongda (Governor) of Gasa, one of the regions of Bhutan. He has now retired and works as an author. In an inspiring conversation, he shared with me how he, with his Buddhist and Bhutanese approach to life, looks at creativity.

He said: 'In Buddhism, the ultimate goal (in life) is to understand who you are. Our ultimate objective in life is to know ourselves. Creativity is one tool for reaching that understanding. Any creative act you do is a way of getting to know yourself'.

I had to repeat that last part out loud after I heard it.

'Any creative act you do is a way of getting to know yourself'.

His message is profound.

In the West, you often hear people talk about how creativity is a way of 'expressing yourself'. Creativity is seen as us creating something for the world. Making the world better.

But according to Dorji Dhradhul, we have it all backwards.

Yes, creativity is all that, but it is not the main objective of creativity. The main purpose is to use creativity to better understand ourselves.

Or in other words: Creativity is not something from you to the world. It is something from you to you.

It's inward. Not outward.

Or perhaps better put: **'Creativity is not about just expressing yourself. It is a way of discovering yourself'.**

Listening to Dorji, I realise that he is right. True creativity is a journey into your subconscious to find undiscovered gems of your own brilliance. Brilliant gems of you that you were previously not aware of. By finding them, you find more of you.

As a matter of fact, you cannot create anything that is truly creative if it's not a part of who you are. And by exploring your creativity, you are exploring who you really are.

Thinking back to the most creative projects I have been working on in my life, regardless if they have been commercially successful or not, it is clear to me that they have all taught me something about who I truly am.

Stop thinking about creativity as something you do to 'create something', and definitely stop thinking about creativity as something you do to accommodate someone else – be that a client, a market or 'target audience'.

Do not get me wrong, creating for others can bring success, money and fame, but the true meaning of the creative process is something fundamentally different. It's about you learning about yourself.

Why? Well, in the words of Dorji, 'Knowing yourself leads to mindfulness, and mindfulness leads to happiness'.

In our conversation, Mr. Dhradhul also gave me a reminder: 'If creativity is getting to know yourself, then checking in with yourself regularly is essential to staying on the right path'.

What he meant was that many people spend their lives creating things that are not true to who they – at this

moment – are. That kind of creativity is false. It means they are creating for someone else, or for what they think someone else wants. Or for who they used to be. To make sure you are creating something that will help your current you discover something new about who you are, you need to know who you are at this moment. So, make sure to check in with who you currently are.

Remember: The ultimate act of creativity is to discover who you truly are. To learn more about yourself. So go explore yourself.

Reflection

Who are you really? That is not an easy question to answer. To make it a little bit easier to answer, I suggest you try this technique: Think of the last creative project you finished: Most people would evaluate the end result and the process. But I want you to:

(1) Evaluate the result (what you created).

(2) Evaluate the creative process (how you can create something even better in the future).

And finally,

(3) Now *also* evaluate what the creative project *taught* you about yourself (who did you become?).

Most people would skip step 3. That is unfortunate, as it is arguably the most profound one.

Adding the third step will just take you an additional couple of minutes for your evaluation, but do this consistently over time and, you will have created a very powerful habit of self-understanding.

The journey away from ego – that is the
common theme of the previous and the next
section. In Bhutan, I was reminded about going
inwards for creativity. In Vietnam, I was
reminded to let go of ego. Both are gentle
journeys away from ego.

Gentle creativity (Ho Chi Minh City, Vietnam)

When you arrive in Ho Chi Minh City, the word 'gentle' may not be the first word you think of. 'Chaos' might be a more suitable word, as you watch the motorcycles swirl around you in an apparently illogical and crazy way. But you quickly realise that it only looks crazy to your untrained eye. What it actually is is 'gentle'. Just as a group of starlings flying together in a big cloud of birds at first looks chaotic and stressful, but then, the more you observe them, the more you see how beautiful and mesmerising the flow of a murmuration is. The bikes in Ho Chi Minh City are equally mesmerising as each rider adapts to the others, forming a fluid, shifting – yes, gentle – organism of humans in traffic. They are not working against each other – but working together. A murmuration of bikes.

The trick to not being run over in the Ho Chi Minh traffic is not to think, but to feel, and that is, as it turns out, the lesson for creative freedom that I brought back from Vietnam. It is a lesson that came to me in a pottery studio.

Trang Nguyen is the founder of Meow Pottery Workshop, a small pottery studio where tourists and locals come to learn how to make their own cups, vases and plates. Sitting in her studio, she shared with me the most significant issue that beginners in her pottery classes have: They think.

According to Trang, the right approach to creating pottery is not to think. But to feel.

When you overthink something, it leads to expectations. When there are expectations, there will be disappointments. When there are disappointments, there are failures.

Trang: 'People would come to the class and expect to be able to create a specific cup or vase that they had seen on the internet. When they cannot re-create it they get upset. They cry, scream, and throw things on the floor. They think that they have failed, and they are miserable'.

But if there are no expectations, there can be no failure.

Instead of expectations, Trang encourages her students to go for 'acceptance': 'My job (as their teacher) is to get them to understand there is no "failure" – just "acceptance"'.

Acceptance of what comes out of the process. Acceptance of how something turned out.

Instead of thinking about what to create, we should let our creativity lead us. We should not think; we should listen. In the case of pottery, listen to what the clay is telling us. Trang believes that experienced pottery makers are so good at listening to the clay that it feels like they understand each other.

In other words, beginners overthink, the experienced creator feels and the experts understand together with the creative project; they become one with it. For Trang, this means that she cannot create two identical objects, and if someone asks her to make multiple identical cups, for example, she will decline the request. Every time she starts on a new cup, she can have ideas about what to make, but she feels that she is not in sole control of how the projects end up. The cup has ideas of how it wants to be made.

This might sound woo-woo for some reading this, but the idea of 'listening to the creative message' that is coming out of a creative project is something I have heard repeatedly when interviewing creative people.

So how to do that?

'The problem is that people come here to create something that they want others to admire', Trang said to me. 'It is the ego that is talking. We must get rid of that'. Her comment reminded me of a discussion I had with another artist in Saigon: Bam Bi.

Bam Bi (Vo Hoang Phuong Uyen) from B/S Art Studio is a painter and musician who grew up in a family of embroiderers in the famous Mai Anh Dao Valley in Da Lat City in Vietnam. I met with her in Ho Chi Minh City, where she now lives, because I wanted to understand how to master the art of 'gentle creativity'.

Bam Bi is a soft-spoken, unassuming person, so much so that the people who meet her in her gallery that doubles as a café often mistake her for one of the café staff. She is fine with that as she seems to have no ego that is bothering her with thoughts about what others think of her. She is just here to paint, to play her flute and to create – and to teach others to create. In her studio, she teaches her students to paint and to learn about Vietnamese culture.

It is to meet people like Bam Bi that I have arrived in Saigon, as Ho Chi Minh City is still often referred to. To meet with gentle, creative souls with the patience to teach others to create.

When Bam Bi teaches foreigners to create, her first task is to get them to, in her words, 'Open their hearts'. According to her, too many of the people who come to her have their creativity blocked because they lack the ability to set their ego aside. 'They come here with a look on their face as if they know everything. **(To be creative) you need to be ready to have questions. When you have questions, you are ready to listen, and when you are ready to listen, you can get a pure heart. The moment we see the purity of our hearts is the moment we are ready to see the magic of life. Find purity of heart'.**

If you stand long enough and look at the people in Saigon navigate the congested traffic on their motorcycles, you notice the almost non-existent anger, road rage or stress that usually accompany a traffic jam in big cities. People are trying to come home, but not at the expense of others. They have a mindset of gentle collaboration. They feel the traffic.

Gentle people, of course, exist everywhere, but in my experience of travelling the world, Vietnam has a larger concentration of them. It is something with the culture that creates an atmosphere of gentleness. Personally, I feel I become a better person when I am in, or have recently been to, Vietnam. It's as if my energy changes to a softer frequency. And I am usually in a very creative mode at those times. I guess my heart is more open.

Reflection

In the song 'Come from the Heart' Susanna Clark and Richard Leigh wrote the famous lines: 'You've got to sing like you don't need the money,

You've got to love like you'll never get hurt,

You've got to dance like there's nobody watching,

You've got to come from the heart if you want it to work'.

Those are lines about removing your ego. Inspired by their song, we could say **'You've got to create like your ego isn't watching'.**

To remove your ego from the creative process, focus your attention on the actual creative project you are working on. Next time you create something, do not ask 'What do I want to create?', ask 'What wants to be created?' Instead of 'What am I aiming for?', ask 'Let's see where this takes us'.

Creativity is very much about
surrendering – like surrendering your ego to
the creative process (as in the previous section
about gentle creativity) and surrendering to
the fact that your ideas might go against the
very zeitgeist of the time (as we will soon learn
from Manfred in the next section
from Germany).

To Manfred – The act of going against the spirit of the time (Berlin, Germany)

The German language has given us some great words: like *Schadenfreude* (as in the pleasure derived from someone else's misfortune), *Besserwisser* (someone who always thinks they know better than everyone else and insists on correcting others) and *Wanderlust* (the strong urge to travel and explore the world). And then there is *Zeitgeist*, literally translating to 'the spirit (or the ghost) of the time'. Zeitgeist is a very useful word to describe the dominant cultural and intellectual climate of an era, but I would like to introduce you to another German word that is almost the opposite of zeitgeist, and which is perhaps even more important. **That word is 'manfred'.**

Now, technically, 'manfred' is not an existing German word, at least not yet, but I think it should be. Manfred is an eponym, a word named after a person, just like the word 'boycott', which is named after English land agent Charles Boycott, who was socially ostracised in Ireland, or the word 'maverick', which comes from Texas rancher Samuel Maverick, who refused to brand his cattle.

The word 'manfred' is named after the West German pastor Manfred Fischer, who worked at a church just next to the Berlin Wall during the historic days of 1989 when the wall between East and West Berlin fell. Just a few months after Ronald Reagan had stood at Brandenburg Gate and told Gorbachev 'Tear down this wall' the wall did fall. People were dancing on the wall, East Berliners walked over to West Berlin to party, and so-called *Mauerspechte* (or 'Wall Woodpeckers' in English) started to hack away on the wall to make it go away – and perhaps also to get a souvenir to remember this historic event.

In the weeks after the wall fell, people wanted it gone. Most people outside of Germany do not understand how big the structure blocking East and West Berlin was: it stretched for more than 150 kilometers and the wall was more than just 'a wall' – it included concrete barriers, watchtowers, anti-vehicle trenches and a heavily guarded 'death strip' to prevent escapes from East to West.

For decades, the wall was a symbol of death. At least 140 people died trying to cross the wall, and for hundreds of thousands, if not millions, of people it was an obstacle that stopped them from reaching freedom. It is quite understandable that people of the time wanted the wall to be demolished as soon as possible in November of 1989.

The zeitgeist was that the wall had to go. After all, it was a symbol of the landscape of death that had brought so much misery over the years, and in December of 1989, the government did take the decision to remove it.

But a few people, such as pastor Manfred Fischer, saw it differently. They had the ability to see beyond the prevailing sentiment of their time and realised that the wall could be transformed from a symbol of death to a monument to remind, and to caution, humanity about the dangers of building walls that separate us. Manfred was able to persuade the soldiers who were assigned to tear down the wall to stop, and he began an intensive lobbying campaign to preserve some of the wall as a monument.

In a video from the time, Pastor Manfred explains, 'If we succeed in keeping this ensemble as a memorial, we hope to show a very tangible spot at which one has tried to separate people who belong together'. And Manfred succeeded. The section of the wall next to his church was saved and today the Berlin Wall Memorial is not just one of Berlin's most visited tourist attractions but also a concrete symbol of how building a concrete wall can divide us.

Today, it seems like an obvious idea to keep the wall, but at the time, it was not. This ability, to see further than the majority's opinion at the time – and to stand up against their point of view and to fight for what is right in the long run – is what I think we should now call 'to manfred', as a tribute to Manfred Fischer.

Creativity is often seen as zigging when everyone else is zagging. But in reality, it is about manfredding when everyone is zeitgeisting. Creativity is not just about doing things opposite of what everyone is doing, but to do it differently than everyone else because you see something that others are not seeing.

I learned about Manfred Fischer and his fight for the wall during a visit to Berlin where I met with Professor Axel Klausmeier of The Berlin Wall Foundation. Between 2001 and 2003, he documented the remains of the Berlin Wall on behalf of the Berlin Senate and since January 2009, he has been Director of the Berlin Wall Foundation. The Berlin Wall Foundation preserves the architectural remains of the wall and helps convey their history in the context of the Cold War and enables the victims to be commemorated. During our conversation, which took place in a room where we could look out over the preserved wall, he discussed the foresight of Manfred Fischer and the other few people who fought for the preservation of the wall. Visiting the preserved wall after my meeting with

Professor Klausmeier, I could see parents explaining the wall's significance to their children, the wall serving as a powerful and pedagogical symbol – and warning – of the darkness of human behaviour. Not a single person there could even imagine arguing against tearing the wall down. For that, we should be grateful to Manfred and his colleagues.

They saw what no one else saw at the time, and they realised that their uncomfortable position was worth fighting for because the zeitgeist would change.

Reflection

Write down all the ways that the idea you are working on is different from what others are doing. Next, write down what value there is in doing that difference. Finally, write down *why* it is important to you that this difference is there.

From a pastor in Berlin, we listened to the
story of seeing beyond what others see.
In Mumbai, we will listen to a story about
seeing beyond our own current situation.
Our teachers will be the most unlikely of
teachers for a creativity book: the children of
sex workers in the slums. Turns out they have
an important message for the rest of us.

Sufferrender (Kamathipura, Mumbai, India)

Just one hour before I went to the slum of Kamathipura and met with the girls of Kranti, I had been attending a conference at the Taj hotel in Mumbai, where I had spoken in front of the leaders of some of India's largest companies. At the conference I had, amongst other things, interviewed some CEOs and spoken to a woman from the Indian space program about their latest innovations, like how they sent a probe to Mars on a budget smaller than some Hollywood films about space. From interviewing CEOs and space experts to meeting with children living in the slum on the same day – that is what exploring creativity is all about. And it was not meeting with the CEOs, or the woman from the space programme, that had the biggest impact on me that day. It was meeting the girls. **If you are curious about humanity, you will be open to learning from and listening to anyone – regardless of their position, age or background.** I am very happy I decided to also go and listen to the girls of Kranti. The Kranti girls' approach to life changed how I approached my own. And now I hope it will make you reevaluate how you look at things.

The Hindi word 'kranti' translates to 'revolution', but it can also mean personal or intellectual transformation. It is the very suitable name taken by the NGO Kranti based in Mumbai.

Kranti works with the children of sex workers in the slums of Mumbai. On the social ladder of society, you probably cannot start off lower than the people Kranti is determined to help. Uneducated. Girls. Of sex workers. In the slums. Of India.

I had decided to meet with Robin Chaurasiya, one of the passionate people behind Kranti, to learn more about their work and to see if I could learn something about creativity from people who normally would not be interviewed about their views on that subject.

It would turn out to be a meeting that would change me to the core.

When I met with Robin, Kranti was housed in a tiny and bare apartment with almost no furniture, where about a dozen girls both lived and got their education. As an NGO, Kranti does not have a lot of resources, but what they lack in money, they make up for with creativity, passion, love and grit. What they are able to achieve is nothing short of amazing. The staff of Kranti are determined to show that any person's life can blossom if they are given a chance and some help.

Kranti helps young girls get off the streets of the red-light district, gives them a safe place to stay and provides them with an education. (When I was there, they were watching TED Talks on an iPad. After watching the talks, they then discussed the topic that had been covered in the speech.)

Some of the girls have had astonishing transformations. Like Sandhya, who recently graduated with a master's degree in Gender and Peace Building from the UN University for Peace. Or Mahek, who went on to study theatre in the United States and even got to perform in a Broadway play.

During my visit, I got to discuss the girls' views on creativity and life and they introduced me to a concept they chose to call: 'Sufferender'. **Sufferender is a word that they made up during our conversation, and it is a combination of the words 'suffer' and 'surrender'.** (These teenage girl's native language is, obviously, not English, and I am aware that the made up word they came up with is a bit 'clunky', but I decided to honour the word they coined, both to keep the authenticity of the story, but also because the meaning of the world becomes stronger if I keep their original idea instead of trying to edit it.)

Sufferender means to surrender to your situation in the moment, but to not surrender to suffering, nor give up. And then they gave me a few examples of what they meant.

They told me that before they lived at Kranti, they were forced to stay up all night out in the streets as their mothers were working in their homes. It was too dangerous for them to sleep in the streets so instead the girls would gather in groups, light a fire and then sit around the fire and sing.

The act of sufferendering was to accept that they would have to be awake all night, but not let that stop them from creating a better situation by singing together.

Robin chipped in and told me about one time when Kranti had gotten a sponsor to fly a group of girls from Kranti to Europe to walk a pilgrimage route from France to Spain. When they arrived in France, Robin had to tell the girls that they did not have enough money to make the full walk, but the girls just said, 'Let's walk as long as we can and enjoy that'. As they walked, they would approach fellow pilgrims and explain that they had no money. In the end, they got so much money that they could finish the full walk. Surrender to your situation (we are poor), but not to the suffering (we might have to give up too early), and do not let that make you give up (we will keep walking and enjoying the walk as long as we can).

As I was listening to the girls explain their approach to life with big smiles and sparkling eyes, I not only reevaluated how I thought about people living in the slums, but also my own approach to life. One of the girls looked at me and said: 'You (in the rich world) have everything, mobile phones, a roof over your head, a job and money – and yet you are miserable. Why?' She exemplified with a wanna-be actress working as a waiter in New York: 'She will be miserable because she wants to be an actress, but now she is "just" a waitress. She defines herself as a "struggling actress". Instead, she should think of herself as a great waitress who has ambitions and drive to become a great actress one day'.

Surrender to your situation (right now you are a waitress), but not to the suffering (enjoy being a waitress while working toward your dream of becoming an actress) and do not give up on your dream (of one day becoming an actress).

The girls of Kranti showed me the power of mental reframing. Creativity thrives in a positive mind. Last I heard from Robin, they had been evicted from their place in Kamathipura so Kranti took that as an opportunity to move to the Himalayan foothills where they bought their own 4-storey house and where they now host 30 new Krantikaris, ages 8–20, from red-light areas across India.

Reflection

What negative self-talk is blocking you from creating a better life for yourself?

How could you reframe that story in your head into a positive message while still being true to the situation?

We leave the slums of Mumbai for a short flight to Sri Lanka. We are here to reflect on change, and our story begins just as we land.

Reading the tea leaves of change (Colombo, Sri Lanka)

The first time I came to the beautiful island of Sri Lanka was more than 20 years ago. I did not get a good first impression. To go through immigration, we had to wait for more than three hours in the warm and humid, non-airconditioned arrival hall while the immigration officers painstakingly slowly let people into the country. Finally, I walked up to an officer and told him, 'This is a terrible way of welcoming someone to your country, you should make passport controls faster'. The man, who was wearing a machine gun (this was during the civil war in the country), replied unfazed: 'I have been to England, there is a three-hour waiting line at Heathrow too ...'. And yes, he did have a point; Heathrow has been known for terrible service as well.

Many years later, I arrived back in Colombo again, and this time they had opened a new, airconditioned, airport. Immigration was just three minutes. I walked up to the guy in charge and congratulated him for the fast and friendly service and he replied: 'Yes, we are trying some new innovations here'.

It is a mystery to me how so many countries can make arrival in a country such a bad experience. **First impressions matter and, honestly, most countries mess it up.** The biggest mystery is, perhaps, why more countries do not change when they notice how other countries' immigration procedures improve.

The change in attitude of the Sri Lankan immigration service, and the positive changes it created for visitors to Sri Lanka, still make me smile. It's a story about how positive human change is possible when we are ready to question how things are done and open to trying new ways.

But while we are in Sri Lanka, let's also share a cautionary tale about people's inability to change.

This story was told to me by one of my former employees, Ayachana. During one of her trips through her country, she visited the tea-growing region and toured one of the tea plantations.

During the tour, they were shown the tea drying stations where huge drying machines remove the moisture from the leaves. Ayachana noticed that the drying machines were kept on the second floor of the building, forcing the workers to walk up a steep step of stairs with heavy bags of tea on their backs.

When she inquired why the drying machines were not placed on the ground floor, the guide – in a matter-of-fact tone of voice – replied: 'Drying has always been done on the second floor, because the breeze is stronger here'.

Yes, in the olden days it made sense to dry leaves on a floor that was higher up to take advantage of the stronger breeze there, but when the drying is done by machines that – of course – doesn't matter anymore, but the tea workers were so stuck in the idea that 'tea is dried where the breeze is stronger' that they were unable to see that drying leaves on the second floor was suddenly now a bad idea.

To not change even when it would make our world better, in a way, goes against the whole Theory of Evolution. But we humans are paradoxes – we are the most innovative species in the known universe, and yet we can be so utterly stuck in our ways. **Being stuck in how things 'have' to be done is stopping us from reaching our creative potential. It's a disease. Developing one's creativity is the cure.**

Sri Lanka has a special place in my heart. I must have been to the country more than 30 times over the span of the last 20+ years. Islands, in general, attract me. People talk about how an 'island mentality' is something negative. How living on an island makes you insular. I think that is unfair. I think people who live on islands are just as likely to have an open and explorative mindset as anyone else. Maybe more so. To me, 'island mindset' means 'open to explore'. As an islander, you are reminded that there is a different world out there every time you look out at the sea. Or as Moana sings in the animated Disney movie 'See the line where the sky meets the sea. It calls me ...'

I guess there are two kinds of island people: The ones who look at the water as a wall, and the ones who look at the water as an invitation.

Reflection

Inspired by the two stories from Sri Lanka, look up from this book and take a good look at the world around you. What outdated practices are the companies behind your everyday products and services still following, long after they should have adopted new technologies or solutions? Pick five products and services and identify where they are being obstinate, in other words, where they are stubbornly refusing to upgrade their behaviour. Make a list of the things you notice. The point with this is not to let those companies know (we both know that they probably will not change even if you inform them about what you have noticed), the point is for you to then write down your analysis for why these companies *haven't changed* – despite the fact that they clearly should. Then see if you can find patterns for why needed change is not happening. By identifying other companies' inabilities to change, you will hopefully learn something about your own inabilities too. Then, when you are warmed up, tackle this question: **What does your own industry keep doing just because it has always been doing it, and what processes are already so archaic that you need to remove them today?**

To reach our creative potential, we need to let go of our old ways. That is a message that needs to be repeated. But to reach our full creative potential, we need to let go of trying to understand it.

In the beginning of this book, I wrote 'You cannot master that which you do not understand'. That is true. But it is also true that to fully master creativity, we have to surrender to the idea that we cannot fully understand it. We have to surrender to it.

This paradox of mastery through surrender is something I discussed with an artist in Riga.

Receive the mystery (Riga, Latvia)

As much as we would like to think we can understand it, we should come to peace with the idea that some aspects of the creative process are a mystery.

A mystery, as in 'something that is difficult or impossible to understand or explain'.

That does not mean we should give up on the idea of trying to study it, or that we should not try to explore it. (I have, after all, been trying to explore creativity for the last 25+ years, so clearly, I am a fan of doing just that.)

But it does mean that the core of creativity is beyond our conscious understanding. And we should approach creativity from that perspective.

Ērika Kumerova, a Latvian painter, calls this mindset 'Receiving the mystery'.

I met with Erika at one of the many cafés located at the Latvian seaside resort of Jūrmala. With its 33 kilometers stretch of white-sand beach and its art nouveau wooden buildings, Jūrmala has attracted artists, as well as party goers and vacationers for centuries.

Over a cup of coffee and a glass of juice, I asked Erika how she approaches a new painting to better understand her creative process. She said: 'Every artwork is an act of discovering. I paint intuitively. Sometimes I don't know what (the painting) is going to be. I just grab some paint and some tools, and I trust my hands. I trust that they will lead me somewhere. The artwork leads you, it tells you what to do next'.

You could say that Erika surrenders to the process.

Standing at an empty canvas, she will just look at all the colour tubes lying there in front of her and pick up the tubes that feel right at that moment and pour their colour onto the canvas.

Erika: 'I have to feel inside of me for what is right. You know how, when you are trying to go to sleep in bed, you know which side you want to lie on? It's the same feeling'.

The keyword here is 'feeling'.

To feel the right colour. Erika agrees: 'I am totally not thinking at this point. I would say it's a mystery because sometimes, even when I look at my work, I don't know how I did that. I don't know how that happened. I cannot repeat it again. It's impossible'.

Creativity, to Erika, is about listening. Listening to the Universe. To something un-understandingly larger than ourselves.

Something so powerful that we cannot comprehend it by just thinking. But something we can still tap into. I asked Erika how to do that:

Erika: 'It's like the antennas of an ant. You have to feel'.

And what do antennas do?

They receive.

So, **creativity is about receiving. Receiving the Mystery.** To be open enough, present enough, humble enough to invite the idea into yourself.

I ask Erika to describe the three rules for Receiving the Mystery.

She said:

'Rule number 1: Turn off your thinking.

Rule number 2: Keep going. Do not stop. Even when you feel that you don't know what to do, just trust yourself and keep going. The process has to happen'.

And then she added:

> 'The third rule is again the first rule. Because that thinking comes back all the time. And you need to stop it'.

Thinking of the creative process as a mystery that is there for you to receive removes you from the pressure. Think of how a fisherman will pick the right place to fish but then surrender to the process and patiently wait for the fish to bite. There is very little he can do, so he does nothing. He just waits. And so should you. Trust that it will come.

And then suddenly the idea arrives, just like how the fish suddenly bites and the float of the fisherman's line goes under water. That moment is when you suddenly see a path. When you become consciously aware of what your subconscious has known for a while.

Erika reflects on those moments and said to me: 'When the ideas come, it's like total happiness. You do not need any drugs. This is better'.

As we are finishing our drinks outside the café, Erika comes back to how important it is to reduce the thinking aspect of the creative process.

She said: 'You have to feel how the paint flows, you have to listen to the sound of the brush, is it telling you to make longer strokes or ...'

This process of waiting for the Universe to put the idea inside of you is something that almost every creative person I have interviewed knows and recognises, but very few have been able to describe. Because it is difficult to put into words.

And perhaps it should be.

Because, if we became too good at describing and defining it, then the mystery would be gone. And that is the last thing we want.

Instead of trying to demystify the mystery of creativity, embrace it.

Reflection

Pause for a minute and just sit in the moment and wait.

Longer. Do it longer than you thought you should. At least ten times longer. Just pause, sit in the moment and wait.

What did you receive?

The seventh creative continent: Cultural creative inspiration

Insights into different ways of thinking around creativity from around the globe.

Copying right (Beijing, China)

It was the most peculiar book fair I have ever attended: Instead of having booths in a convention hall, each publisher had been given a hotel room where they would feature their new books by placing them on the hotel room beds. The attendees at this book fair would walk from room to room to look for titles they might be interested in. It was very crowded, very sweaty and – frankly – very weird. **But, then again, this was Beijing in 2005, and China was in a rush to become a 'creative country' and so the country did a lot of unconventional things.** I had just arrived in China, and I was amazed. The Chinese attending the fair thought making book deals on beds filled with books was totally normal.

I had moved to China to better understand Chinese creativity and to help publish and promote my books in the Chinese market. In 2005, China had just launched a new 5-Year Plan where the word 'Innovation' was mentioned more than 70 times. The Middle Kingdom was going all-in on transforming itself into a creative and innovative country, and as an author of creativity books, I wanted to be part of that journey.

I attended this particular book fair to find the right publisher for the Mandarin version of my book 'The Idea Book'. As I was wandering through the halls of the hotel, going in and out of rooms filled with hundreds of books on beds, I saw a publisher promoting a book with the title 'Blue Sea Strategy' written in English on the otherwise Chinese cover. I assumed it was an adapted way of writing 'Blue Ocean Strategy' in slightly easier-to-understand English.

At the time, the book *'Blue Ocean Strategy'* was the most successful book on corporate innovation. The main message of *Blue Ocean Strategy* is the need to create new, unique markets (aka 'blue oceans') where there's no competition, instead of fighting over customers in crowded, competitive markets (aka 'red oceans') where everyone is 'bleeding' by competing for the same customers with the same products. *Blue Ocean Strategy* has now sold more than 4 million copies worldwide and has been translated into 49 languages.

To get the same publisher as the authors of *Blue Ocean Strategy* would be a big win for any author of creativity books, so when I saw the book there on the bed that had the English title *'Blue Sea Strategy'* I approached the publisher and started to compliment them on being able to get the Chinese rights to such a successful book. The publisher looked a bit uncomfortable. I continued to praise the book, while trying to get them interested in my book, until the Chinese publisher quietly explained that the book they were selling was not the translated version of *Blue Ocean Strategy*, it was a Chinese rip-off book entitled *'Blue Sea Strategy'* ...

They had essentially written a book all about the need to stand out and to not compete on having the same offering as others – and they had done so by shamelessly copying everything from an international bestseller with the message about the need to create unique markets.

This is a funny, but oh so common, story about 'creativity' in China in the early 2000s. It's not difficult to find many other examples of blatant copying. Like the Chinese coffee shop

'Bucksstar Coffee', or the pizza chain 'Pizza Huh', a cookie brand called 'Borio' and a beer brand called 'Cerono Extra' ... There are not only examples of fake iPhones in China, but also of fake Apple Stores selling those phones.

Then there is the fake London Tower Bridge over the Yuanhe Pond in Suzhou, Jiangsu Province, and the gated community in Tianducheng, Hangzhou, with a 108-metre-tall replica of the Eiffel Tower. In other parts of China, there is, for example, a copy of the Leaning Tower of Pisa in Shanghai and a replica of the Kremlin in Mentougou outside of Beijing. The list just goes on and on and on.

Perhaps the most mind-blowing example is how developers have built copies of whole European towns in China. Like how a Chinese town in Songjiang is a copy of the English town Thames Town, complete with cobblestone streets, Victorian terraces, corner shops and red telephone boxes. The Chinese town of Guangdong is a copy of the Austrian town of Hallstatt with everything from a replica church clock tower to European-style wooden houses. And the Chinese town of Luodian New Town just outside Shanghai copied the cute little Swedish town of Sigtuna, including a copy of Lake Mälaren – in Luodian called 'Meilan Lake'.

Learning about all these examples of Chinese rip-offs of Western brands, it could be very easy to write off creativity from China.

As a matter of fact, the question: 'What could we possibly learn about creativity from China? After all, all they do is copy?', was, for years, the most common comment I got when

I told people that I used to live in China to study the Chinese approach to creativity.

It's easy to dismiss Chinese creativity by citing these examples of 'bad copies' of Western ideas and to, with a smirky smile, say: 'See, all they do in China is copy us'.

But that would be a big mistake.

Because creativity is very much about copying. Not copying straight off, but the creative process feeds on copying. Every idea ever conceived is a combination of already existing ideas. It's easy to see in, for example, the idea of creating the drink Gin & Tonic, which is a combination of the previously known things 'gin' and 'tonic'. Or the invention of the 'peanut butter and jelly sandwich' which is a combination of the previously known things like sandwich, peanut butter and jelly. But not only is every recipe a combination of existing ingredients, as a matter of fact, *every* idea is a combination of previously existing ideas. The iPhone, when it came, while being seen as an amazing innovation, is actually 'just' a combination of the concept of a mobile telephone and a computer. Apple under Steve Jobs was generally regarded as a powerhouse of innovation, but Jobs, for example, 'stole', or copied, the concept of the graphical interface – and the computer mouse – from a visit to Xerox PARC. And so on.

It is, in fact, impossible to think of an idea that is not a combination of previously known ideas. Isaac Newton, the man who famously discovered, amongst other things, the concept of gravity, knew this. That is why he, in a letter to Robert Hooke in 1675, wrote: 'If I have seen further (than others) it is by standing on the shoulders of giants'.

Funnily enough, it seems that Isaac Newton had copied this famous quote about standing on giants – the first mention of the quote can be found more than 500 years earlier when, 1123, William of Conches wrote: 'The ancients had only the books which they themselves wrote, but we have all their books and moreover all those which have been written from the beginning until our time … . Hence, we are like a dwarf perched on the shoulders of a giant'.

Isaac Newton was a creative genius, but without Galileo Galilei, Nicolaus Copernicus and all the creative 'giants' before him, there would be no Isaac Newton. **Everyone copies someone, or something.**

When we realise that all creative activity is grounded in picking inspiration from other, already existing ideas, then we realise that all creative activity includes some aspect of copying.

The trick is *how* you copy.

Creative people copy in unexpected ways, find inspiration where others do not look. Connect the seemingly un-connectable. Let their subconscious mind combine seemingly uncombinable – is that a word? – things in the most unexpected way. But they still copy.

This notion that all ideas are inspired by previous ideas can be very provocative for some people. But if you lower your guard and think about it, you will come to the realisation that it is true. 'How about the wheel?', people will sometimes ask me. Before the wheel, people used logs. The wheel is 'just' a chopped-off log … 'How about the computer?' The history of the computer and the binary system that it runs on is an excellent example of 'standing on the shoulders of giants'.

In 1946, John Mauchly and J. Presper Eckert built ENIAC, one of the first general-purpose electronic digital computers. But they did that thanks to the work of, amongst many others, Alan M. Turing, who provided the mathematical foundation of modern computing when he created the Turing machine. Turing stood on the shoulders of Charles Babbage, who, with his Difference Engine and Analytical Engine, built mechanical devices that embodied many principles of modern computing; and of Ada Lovelace, who is often regarded as the first computer programmer. Ada wrote detailed notes and created the first published algorithm intended for Babbage's Analytical Engine.

But without the work of Gottfried Wilhelm Leibniz, who at the end of the 17th century developed the binary number system, there would be no Ada Lovelace or Charles Babbage innovations. And Gottfried Wilhelm Leibniz was helped in his creative work of inventing the binary system by correspondence with Jesuit missionaries working in China, who told him about I Ching, an old Chinese book from the 9th century BCE which includes passages describing ideas around a binary system based on the Taoist duality of yin and yang. **Gottfried was standing on the shoulders of some very old Chinese giants and the idea of the most modern of computers can be traced back to ideas from more than two thousand years ago in Asia.** And with this short history lesson, we are now back to China and creativity.

Because, while we can laugh at the silly copying practices of some Chinese, we should also learn from and be inspired by how other Chinese copy. From automotive to mobile games to Internet services or the use of technology at restaurants – in many areas Chinese companies are now more innovative and creative than their Western competitors. And their secret lies in their ability to copy.

When I was living in China, I met a very creative young lady called Amelia who put words on the mindset of Chinese creativity. She told me: 'You Westerners are obsessed with creativity. It's all you talk about. You talk about intellectual property, patents and copyright. Listen to me, Fredrik: **It's not about "copyright" – it's about "copying right"**!'

It's not about 'copyright' – it's about 'copying right'.

This is brilliant.

Creativity is to have the ability to combine already existing ideas in an unexpected way. To copy right. Not to copy wrong, copying wrong is, well, wrong. Not to copy sloppily. But to copy right.

And there is the insight: It is much easier for someone who has been copying wrong to learn how to copy right, than it is for someone to become creative who thinks that all creativity is 100% unique and totally uninspired by previous ideas.

Whilst many people in the West take pride in not looking at what others are doing, the Chinese have been travelling around the world to look at what everyone is doing and then perfected the art of copying right.

We should copy more, but we should copy right. That is the lesson in creativity from China. Or in the words of T.S. Eliot's **'Immature poets imitate. Mature poets steal'.**

Reflection

Who could you copy right?

Who is doing something in an amazing way that you can take inspiration from and tweak so that the essence of that idea is best implemented into what you are doing, while at the same time making sure that you are not plagiarising or losing what is authentically you?

May I suggest:

Pick three creators in your own industry whom you admire. Pick one of their creations that inspires you the most. First, copy it straight off as best you can (the whole piece or a sample of it). Note what you learned from doing that.

Second, copy only the essence of those other creators' ideas. Reflect on what made their ideas inspire you so much and copy just the essence of that. Note what you learned from doing that.

Third, create an original piece but incorporate some of that essence into it. Note what you learned from doing that.

Creativity is abundance. Do not settle for just your own ideas – also copy right the best from others, as we learned from Amelia in Beijing. Do not settle for just one plan – have multiple plans to give you an abundance of options, as we will learn from the creative people in Nigeria.

Deviated Thinking – The art of being able to simultaneously juggle many alternative solutions (Lagos, Nigeria)

When I arrive at the Lagos International airport, it's past midnight. I turn on my phone to look for the number of the driver I had been assigned. As I open WhatsApp, I have messages from two people, both claiming to be my drivers. Both are using my name, and both say there has been a change in the planning so that the driver I have been assigned cannot come and instead they will send a new driver. One of these messages is a scam. (Fake drivers pretending to be there to pick you up is an elaborate scam in airports around the world.)

Nigeria should be better known for its positive creativity. This African giant – one in every five Africans is a Nigerian, and the median age of the country is just 18.1 years.

Nigeria is bustling with creative energy and it is only ignorance from uninformed and uninterested people outside of Africa that is stopping more great Nigerian creativity from going global. I have been to Lagos on multiple occasions. I go back because every time I go, I get revitalised, and to learn more from its young and dynamic population. **Some might say Lagos is chaotic – I would use the word vibrant.**

Growing up in this vibrant chaos creates a special kind of mentality.

Olande Atere, Chief Customer Experience Officer at one of Nigeria's biggest banks, calls this way of thinking 'Deviated Thinking'. It's a mindset of constantly having multiple alternative plans for what you are trying to achieve.

A Nigerian Robert Frost could have penned a poem that would read: **'Two roads diverged in a yellow wood, and I–I kept the other one as an option. And that has made all the difference'.**

Of course, people everywhere will have back-up plans, but over a cup of tea at the Palace Hotel in Lagos, Olande Atere explained how Nigerians think: 'It's not about having a back-up plan just in case, it's about having multiple alternative plans because you know you will probably need them'.

Not options 'just in case' but options 'just because'.

Lars Johannisson, the CEO of RackCentre, is a Swedish entrepreneur who runs a data centre in Lagos, whom I met on the same trip, agrees: 'Nigerians always have a plan B, a plan C and a plan D. It can be frustrating sometimes, but it makes life here dynamic and resilient'.

In Nigerian Pidgin English, the word for 'alternative' is often expressed as 'another option'. For example, the English sentence 'You can choose an alternative' in Pidgin English becomes 'You fit choose another option'. In Deviated Thinking, there are not 'alternatives to the chosen path', there are 'many options on how to achieve one's goals'.

With multiple options on the table at the same time, you become more flexible, less rigid in any specific way. More focused on the goal than on the specific road you had planned to take to get there.

And when you think about it, creativity is very much about having options.

Uncreative people see one way – or worse: no way. Have one plan – or worse, no plan. Seek one solution.

Creative people see many ways. Have alternative plans. Seek the best solutions.

Wingonia Ikpi, the Founder and CEO of Boxonia Blueprint, a film production company based in Lagos, Nigeria, is another creative I discussed this mindset with during one of my energising visits to Lagos. Wingonia is a film enthusiast and passionate storyteller with years of experience in different areas of the entertainment value chain. When I met with her, she said: '(Here in Nigeria) you can wake up one day and the tariff on the mobile phone has doubled, or the government, overnight, hikes up the price of petrol. In a chaotic and randomly changing world, having just one plan is a very ineffective way to live. When we make a film, we do not just have a plan. We have plans for how to back up the backup plan. If everything is going according to plan in a production, I freak out'.

And then she added: Here (in Nigeria), the mindset isn't 'If one door closes, another one opens'. Here, the mindset is **'As one door might close at any time, know which other doors you can open'.**

One of the business leaders I met after having given a keynote speech at the TeXcellence tech conference in Lagos said to me, 'You have to innovate or die', but then he stopped and corrected himself before he rephrased himself: 'You have to innovate to survive'. That correction is subtle, but it puts the light on the Nigerian way of looking for alternatives. Innovate or die is about using creativity to avoid something bad. It's binary. One or zero. **Innovate to survive is about using creativity for something positive. It's about trying anything that will keep you alive.** Innovate to survive is, in essence, the core of the Darwinist thought of 'survival of the fittest' where the one who has the ability to change when change is needed survives and thrives.

Divergent thinking is all about keeping options open for something better.

If I, that night that I landed at Lagos International Airport, had taken the approach that 'my driver will send me a WhatsApp message when I have arrived as planned' and then gone and met up with him, I would have been scammed, robbed or worse. Instead, I kept the options open as multiple messages came in from various people. I held back on what action to take next until I had evaluated the different options that had presented themselves so that I could finally conclude which of the two drivers was my actual driver by asking them a few test questions that only the real driver would know the answer to. This Divergent Thinking got me safely to my hotel.

Reflection

When you embark on a creative project, how many different options do you generally keep in your head at the same time? No matter what your answer is, try generating several alternative options that could work equally well. During the creative process, go back to them to see if it's time to change path.

Forget about having 'a' plan.

Also forget about having a Plan B.

Go for X number of plans, pick the best one based on the current situation and feel the power that not being held down to one path creates.

From the creative confidence of juggling multiple plans inspired by creatives in Lagos to the creative confidence of a Mexico City chef who challenges the familiar just the right amount.

Surprisingly familiar (Mexico City, Mexico)

Is there any specific food that triggers strong positive emotions in you? Like your mother's chicken soup? Most people have a memory like that. Food is so much more for us humans than just nutrients that we put in our mouths. And a meal can be so more than just 'people eating'. It's about connection and community. About belonging. About creating experiences and memories together.

Chefs know this. They know that their job is not merely to 'prepare calories' for people. Going to a restaurant is about other things. **But if food is so connected to old memories and traditions, how do you innovate and create? And what can we learn about creativity from chefs who successfully balance tradition with innovation?**

That is what I wanted to understand by going to Mexico City to visit Jorge Vallejo of Quintonil. Jorge has been cooking for more than 30 years and his restaurant Quintonil has been listed among the World's 50 Best Restaurants lists multiple times. Last year it was ranked #7. Jorge, like many who are the very best in the world at something, is a very humble person. When we met in his restaurant in Miguel Hidalgo in Mexico City, he started off by telling me: 'I consider myself more a cook than a chef. Of course, I run my own business; I run my own kitchen. My job title is chef, but I consider myself a cook'. As in someone who cooks food.

Mexican food, of course, is famous around the world for its amazing tastes delivered by relatively simple and cheap ingredients. I asked Jorge how the country's food has affected the culture of the country and vice versa. He said: 'Mexico is a place where you can eat well and enjoy good food everywhere. You can go to the richest family in Mexico. Or you can go with the poorest family in Mexico, and you will find beans, you will find chilies. You will find tortillas. Our food, I think, makes us more horizontal. Our food makes you feel at home, regardless of where you eat. The ordinary and simple ingredients make you feel safe'.

Mexican food makes you feel at home. It is comfort food, in the best sense of the word 'comfort'.

When I asked Jorge to describe how he looks at food, he said: 'Food can make you feel joy, it can make you feel nostalgic. It gives birth to very strong emotions. Like how you remember a specific part of your life, your grandma's cinnamon buns'.

And it is true. Certain foods, or certain meals, can create some of the strongest memories. Smell and taste are wired directly to the limbic system, especially the amygdala (emotion) and hippocampus (memory). That's why a particular spice or dish can instantly transport you back to childhood or a special place.

And in his restaurant, Jorge plays with this power of food. He does not use fancy or expensive ingredients (like lobster or caviar) like some other star chefs, and he doesn't experiment with high-tech solutions (like Nitro oxygen) like some celebrity chefs; instead, he sticks to local and familiar Mexican ingredients to create a sense of familiarity.

Jorge explained: 'When you enter my restaurant, I want you to feel at home, regardless of whether you are Mexican, American, or Swedish, like you'.

'But', I objected, 'how can you be ranked as one of the best chefs in the world unless you are innovating and doing things differently?'

Jorge: 'I just also have this particular way of seeing things different. I will see a nopal (a prickly Mexican pear cactus) and think about it in a new way. Instead of doing a salad as you can have it in the street, I will, perhaps, make an ice cream out of it. And it will still taste like a cactus. It should be surprisingly familiar'.

Surprisingly familiar.

That was the lesson in creativity from Mexico that we can apply to anyone trying to introduce something new to a market.

Make something that is just familiar, and it is safe, but a bit boring. Not very interesting.

Make something that is just surprising, and it gets your attention, but it risks making you uneasy.

But make something that is surprisingly familiar, and you get something that feels both interesting and friendly.

The trick is to add the surprise without losing the familiarity. I asked Jorge how he does that. He said: 'I think it's like just trying to be myself as much as I can, but a compressed version of myself. It's like being naked'.

The way I understand Jorge, the technique he uses is to stay true to the heritage of the food he is working with and to then infuse just enough of himself to make it his. To make sure he is not showing off, not trying too hard, not changing things for the sake of changing them. To keep the fundamentals of the food he is working with and then adding the essence of who he is.

That way, he gets a dish that is both authentic to its history and authentic to him.

Jorge's approach of surprisingly familiar is hitting the sweet spot for how to excite people with a novelty while making them feel safe with what they already know.

It might sound like an oxymoron to make something surprisingly familiar, but it is not.

When Steve Jobs introduced the iPod nano by suggesting that the tiny pocket that sits inside the front pocket on jeans was there to store the iPod Nano, he not only made the audience get excited about how small it was, but he also made them feel like the iPod Nano had somehow always been in their lives.

Reflection

If you are trying to create something for a market, for someone else to buy, then reflect on the balance between familiarity and surprise. Is there too much surprise? Too little? Too much familiarity? Not enough familiarity?

If you are having trouble doing this analysis by yourself (sometimes we are just too close to what we are creating), then ask a couple of trusted friends or customers to help you out. Ask them to point out the familiar and the surprising.

From hearing about gently challenging the familiar, we will now do just that by going to North Korea for an insight into creativity. North Korea is probably the definition of unfamiliar territory, and Pyongyang might seem like an unlikely – and unlikable – place to study creativity – but if we want to study human creativity, we have to be willing to study it everywhere.

Collective creativity (Pyongyang, North Korea)

First, an important disclaimer: Before I arrived in Pyongyang, I asked a Westerner who had been there many times: 'Teach me something about North Korea that I should know before I go there'. He said: 'North Koreans are just like all other humans. The vast majority of them – just like most of us – want a peaceful and happy life for themselves, their families, their community and for humanity. And then a small group of people are assholes. The problem is that in some countries, the assholes are in charge ...'

This chapter is about how the people and culture of North Korea inspired me to think differently about creativity. In no way should this chapter be seen as any kind of support of, or legitimisation of, the North Korean regime. (Actually, none of the chapters in this book is in any way supportive of any government.) I do not, in any way, condone the current government of North Korea. If I wrote a book about cooking and included a chapter about North Korean cuisine, it would and should not be seen as support of the North Korean government. In the same way I am writing about the North Korean people's views on creativity and how that inspired me to reflect on what creativity could be, I am not writing about, or writing to support, the current North Korean government or their practices.

With that firmly said, let's dive into the lesson I learned, because it is a fascinating one.

When I travel around the world and ask people what country they think is the most creative, I get many different answers.

People will often say the United States, sometimes they will say China, or Switzerland, South Korea, Singapore or Japan, etc. **But when I ask people to name the *least* creative country on the planet, people almost exclusively say 'North Korea'.**

So, what on Earth could we possibly learn about creativity from the people of the Democratic People's Republic of Korea? That is a genuinely valid question. After all, the country is not famous for creativity, innovation or growth, and it's rarely a role model for anything. For example: The GDP per capita of North Korea is just 3.5% of that of South Korea. The country has been an authoritarian dictatorship for more than seven decades. Sadly, it is estimated that 6 out of 10 North Koreans live below the poverty line.

I must admit that for years I was totally uninterested in going to the country to study creativity, but then, one day, I reminded myself that I am 'The Creativity Explorer' and that I should explore human creativity in all its facets, variations and formats, so I booked a visit to this strange land.

And I am happy that I did. Because it turns out that there was a rather powerful lesson to be learnt from the people of North Korea.

Believe it or not, but the Democratic People's Republic of Korea, or DPRK, as the country is formally known, actually stresses creativity. The ideology of the Workers' Party of Korea – the ruling party of DPRK – is called the Juche Idea. The goal of Juche is to 'establish a self-reliant state that independently determines its political, economic, and military affairs'. In the book '*On the Juche Idea*', former North Korean leader Kim Jong Il talks about the philosophical principle of Juche and how it is 'a man-centered philosophy'. It states that 'Man has independence (자주성,Chajusong), consciousness [ko](의식성,Uisiksong) – and – creativity [ko](창조성, Changjosong)'.

In other words, according to the guiding ideology of North Korea, 'creativity' is one of the three fundamental things that make us human. Who would have thought?

That is interesting, but what I found much more interesting was how they look at what creativity is.

I have now been to North Korea twice and spent a total of more than two weeks in the country. My trip included the usual tourist attractions of visiting the Fatherland Liberation War Victory Memorial Hall, the Mansu Hill Grand Monument, showcasing the giant bronze sculptures of Kim Il-sung and Kim Jong-il, and the Juche Tower. I also got to go and visit the DMC from the North Korean side, go to a local water park (!) and visit a restaurant where dog meat was on the menu. But I also got to speak at a government conference where I had a chance to interact with, talk to – and drink with – local business leaders and government officials. In 30 years of public speaking, I have never had a group that asked more intriguing questions. They really wanted to take the opportunity to learn from the outside world. One thing that stayed in my memory was how, after the conference, all the 200+ attendees spent a minimum of 30 minutes writing page after page of evaluation of each speaker.

It is hard to describe in words what visiting North Korea was like, partly because it is like no other place on Earth.

Partly because you constantly feel like you are being watched, and you never know if what you see is real or staged. It's like being a visitor to the made-up world in the movie 'The Truman Show' with a hint of 'Squid Game' thrown in.

Because North Korea is so hard to wrap one's head around, it took until the last day of my second visit for me to find the insight around creativity that I had been looking for. It happened during a visit to the Mass Games. The Mass Games is a gymnastics and artistic festival hosted at the Rungrado 1st of May Stadium in Pyongyang. Think of it like an opening ceremony for the Olympic Games – just without the Olympic Games. It is ironic that an insight into how to think about being creative came while watching a propaganda event for an authoritarian regime, but creative insights work in mysterious ways.

The Mass Games performance starts off with a card stunt, or a Tifo, where 30,000 schoolchildren, sitting in the stands opposite the audience, hold up different coloured cards to create giant animated mosaic pictures in sync with music. Then, after about 10 minutes, out on the field come thousands and thousands of performers, like 2,000 girls with pom-poms, or 700 boys doing taekwondo in front of a giant North Korean flag, and so on.

It's called The Mass Games for a reason: all the performances are made up of huge groups of people. There is never a solo performer. It's a huge propaganda event for the government.

After the show, I asked my guide – ok, let's be honest: it was 'my' spy – 'How many people were performing in this show?'

He said: 'Oh, more than 50,000'.

When I expressed scepticism about the large number, he insisted, it was indeed more than 50,000 people performing.

That's when it hit me: as soon as the performers came out on the main stage, I had forgotten about the 30,000 schoolchildren holding up their cards in the background. My Western brain was so used to celebrating the 'creative genius on the stage' that as soon as performers came out on the 'main' stage, I *forgot* about the 30,000 children performing in the stands.

While many in the West think of creativity as an individual skill, the approach to creativity in North Korea is more collective. One of my new North Korean friends told me about a North Korean saying that goes: 'One plus one doesn't equal two. One plus one equals "big one"'. She exemplified with clay: 'If you have two pieces of clay and you join them together, you do not have "two clays", you have "one big clay"'.

With this way of thinking, creativity is not something 'I am' doing. It is something 'we are' doing. Together.

They think about creativity like we think of communication, something that happens between humans, not inside just one.

The Nobel Prize is the perfect example of how we in the West tend to look at creativity and innovation as an individual skill. Alfred Nobel, in his will, wrote: '(The Nobel Prize) should go one part to **the person** who made the most important discovery or invention in the field of physics (and chemistry, medicine, literature and peace)'. (Text bolded by me.)

In other words: The prizes should go to the Creative Genius.

If Alfred Nobel had instead travelled to North Korea and gotten inspired to have a more collective approach to creativity, then perhaps the will would have read:

'(The Nobel Prize) should go to the person who made the most important discovery or invention in the field of physics (and chemistry, medicine, literature and peace) – and that person needs to give away 50% of the prize money to all the people who helped him or her win the Nobel Prize'. Because no matter how much of a creative genius you are, you had help in becoming a Nobel Prize laureate. Alfred Nobel could have encouraged the collective mindset by having the winners give away half of their prize money to their first professor, their parents, their competitors, their doctoral students or whoever helped them win that prize.

Outside of North Korea, the industry that has been best at applying a collective mindset to creativity is the movie industry. At the end of the film, the moviemakers will show the name of every single person who worked on the movie, from the director and actors to the stuntmen, the producers and the assistant production accountants, the visual effects supervisor, etc. Even the caterer will get her name in the end credits. Why? Because movie makers know that a movie is created by a huge number of creative people creating together. **All, literally, deserve credit.**

Recently, the mega star Taylor Swift showed an understanding of collective creativity when she announced that all the truck drivers on her Eras Tour in America were given a $10,000 bonus. The truck drivers will never get any appreciation from the fans, and neither will the people selling merchandise, doing security or selling tickets, etc. But Taylor

Swift knows that without all these unsung heroes there would be no show.

Visiting North Korea, I learned that, done wrong, collectivity can create a horrible social construct. But it is also true that, done right, collectivity can create a beautiful common approach to creativity where creativity is something we do together. That was my insight from watching 50,000 North Koreans perform at the mass games. We could call it a Mass Insight.

Reflection

Let's play a little game: Let's say – for the sake of argument and to trigger your imagination – that the Nobel Prize Committee decides to create a new Nobel Prize in Creativity and that they decide to give it to you. And let's also assume that they have been inspired by this chapter and included a new clause in the rules of the prize that the recipient must give away half of the prize money to the people who helped you win the prize.

Then who would you share the prize money with? And why?

And while we are at it: perhaps you should take the time to write to those people and thank them for helping you become the creative person that you are.

Oh, and one more thing: the next time you award or acknowledge someone for a creative task that they have done, think about whether there are others who should also be rewarded. People who were instrumental to the success but who, for some reason, did not easily get recognised.

From an insight about the importance of
shared creative credit that came from the most
unexpected of places for a creativity
book – North Korea – to the advice to seek
creative wisdom that will come from the most
familiar of places for me: Sweden.

It will be our last stop on this voyage around
The World of Creativity. Fittingly enough, the
chapter includes a message to travel the world
for ideas.

Humbly confident, or confidently humble. Like a Swede (Stockholm, Sweden)

No matter how you measure the innovative power of a country, Sweden tends to come close to the top. The World Economic Forum (WEF) has recently ranked Sweden as one of the most competitive countries in the world in its Global Competitiveness Report. Sweden has also been at the top of the European Innovation Scoreboard multiple times. And according to The Global Innovation Index (GII), published by the World Intellectual Property Organization (WIPO), Sweden has held the number two or number three position of most innovative country on the planet every year for the last 10 years in a row. Impressive, to say the least. Especially for a country that is so small that it only represents 0.13% of the global population.

So, what is it with this northern European country that makes it so creative and innovative? Some have hinted at the cold and dark winter months that make Swedes hunker down inside to think and reflect. The Swedish government likes to put forward the idea that the country's long-term focus on education and research is the reason. Others point to Sweden's well-developed infrastructure. All these arguments have some merit, but none captures the uniqueness of Swedish creativity.

As a global author and speaker on creativity who happens to come from Sweden, I have often been asked about my views on why my motherland is so creative.

For the longest time, I was not able to answer the question. Frankly, I would rather point to the many things in the Swedish culture and mindset that tend to kill creativity.

Like the consensus mentality – which is very strong in Sweden – and which risks encouraging groupthink and slow decision making. Or the 'lagom mentality' – a Swedish trait of looking for a solution of 'moderation' – which can stifle risk-taking and bold thinking. Or like the very strong impact of the 'Law of Jante', a Scandinavian cultural concept that emphasises collective equality, and is deeply rooted in my country. The law – that, of course, is not an actual law, but a strong unwritten rule – reads: 'You shall not think that you are special'. The Law of Jante has suppressed countless ambitious Swedes and trampled on many Swedish dreams.

But, despite all the things in the Swedish culture that are negative for creativity, one has to acknowledge that the Kingdom of Sweden houses some really creative people. The list of creative Swedes that has made it onto the global stage is quite impressive. From IKEA to Spotify to Ericsson and Volvo. From Alfred Nobel to ABBA, and many more. A country this small should not have this many global companies and innovators.

So, what is the secret ingredient in the recipe that is Swedish innovation?

Turns out I would receive the answer from a Swedish chef.

Let's get one thing clear: Sweden is *not* known for its food. When was the last time you told your partner 'Honey, let's have Swedish tonight'. Right, probably never happened.

If I ask you to think of Swedish food, you are probably thinking of meatballs from IKEA ... How can a small country of just 10 million people, whose only claim to food fame is bad meatballs in a furniture store, win at the Food Olympics?

Because we do.

Actually, Sweden is nothing less than a culinary superpower at international food competitions. For example: At the IKA/ Culinary Olympics, the world's oldest and most prestigious culinary competition, Sweden rocks. The culinary Olympics have been conducted every four years since 1900. More than 1,800 participants from 67 countries competed in 2024. How did Sweden do? They finished fourth. In 2020, they finished second. In 2012, 2004 and 2000, Sweden won it.

In other words, Sweden consistently ranks as one of the top culinary nations in the world. How on Earth is that possible?

I got the opportunity to meet with the culinary team of Sweden, and they gave me an insight that suddenly gave me clarity on the secret sauce of Swedish creativity. They, in essence, told me:

French chefs often think that French food is the best in the world. After all, 'French cuisine' is a renowned, sophisticated global brand. So French chefs go and study at a 3-star Micheline star-restaurants, convinced they have the best food on the planet. Italian chefs, on the other hand, tend to think that no one really likes French food, and because 'everyone' loves Italian food, they are convinced that they have the best food on the planet. Italian chefs have no interest in studying at a French 3-star Michelin restaurant. Instead, they go and interview their grandmothers about how to make the perfect pasta. Japanese chefs, on the other hand, think that Japan has a superior food culture. After all, it takes more than ten years to become an Itamae – a sushi master chef.

But Swedish chefs know that Sweden doesn't have the best food in the world, so they leave Sweden. They go to Paris to work in a 3-star Michelin restaurant. Then they go to Tokyo – not for ten to twenty years – but perhaps for one or two years to learn from an Itamae. Then they go to Italy and interview one hundred grandmothers about the secret to great pasta. Then they go back to Sweden to learn about meatballs ...

Then they go to the Culinary Olympics and combine all the things they have learned and make, for example, 'Herring sashimi with lingonberry wasabi'. And then they win ...

The secret to Sweden's success at global culinary competitions – and the secret to Sweden's success as a creative country – lies in the Swedes' ability to combine a sense of pride and confidence in their own culture, while at the same time being unusually open and curious to the cultures of others.

To be doubtfully confident.

Or, if you prefer: To be confidently doubting.

Swedes are great at thinking that their country is the greatest country on Earth, while at the same time being experts at thinking that everyone else is better than they are. Tell an American that she is 'unamerican' and she will, most likely, be offended. Same if you tell a Chinese that they are 'unchinese' or an Italian that they are 'unitalian', etc. But tell a Swede that they are 'unswedish' and most Swedes will give you a big grin and reply 'Well, thank you'.

Creativity is about being able to balance confidence with humility. If everyone is walking to the right, you need to be confident to be the only one who walks left. Confidence is crucial for creativity. **But truly creative people are always questioning if what they are doing is right. Perhaps going left is also wrong? Maybe I should go upwards? Or down? Creative people are always doubting.**

The sweet spot for creativity is to be confidently doubting.

Reflection

A sweet spot refers to 'the optimal point or balance in a given situation where conditions are ideal for achieving maximum effectiveness, efficiency, or performance'.

And your 'creative sweet spot' is when you balance the belief in yourself with the disbelief in your own ideas. Get that balance right and your creativity will thrive.

If you want to become more creative, you should assess yourself to see if you are approaching your creative process with a bit too much confidence, or perhaps with a bit too little of it?

On a scale of 1–10, how high would you score your creative confidence?

On a scale of 1–10, how high would you score your creative doubt? (Where 10 is you constantly doubt everything in your creative process.)

For calibration, also ask a trusted friend who knows your creative process well to rate you on the same scale.

If your creative confidence is too low, try to identify where that feeling comes from and what you need to do to fix it. (And write a list of some of the best ideas you have ever had to remind yourself of what you can do.)

If your creative doubt is too low, reach out to someone who is much better than you (there is always someone much better than you) and become a student of someone who is a master at something you are not.

Tweaking your confidence and doubt will help you achieve the creative sweet spot where you balance these opposing creative forces perfectly. Make sure you do it regularly.

The end. And the beginning

We have come to the end of this journey. A journey that had us learn from a hostage negotiator, an a banker and a car designer. We got to listen to children living in the slums and to people suffering from war. Where everything from chefs, artists and dancers to nomads, resort executives and government officials shared their thoughts on the creative process. And many, many more.

We have learnt about creativity from all kinds of humans, and in the process learnt something about humanity through creativity.

If my travels across this beautiful blue planet—to more than 75 countries over more than 25 years—have taught me anything, it is this: everyone cherishes their own creativity, just as they appreciate creativity in others. We just love how it makes us feel, how it makes us grow, how it makes us solve problems and how it makes us express ourselves. How it makes us understand ourselves. How it makes us feel alive.

Perhaps creativity is what makes us human.

And if so, perhaps us becoming more creative could make us more human.

Final reflection

This may be the end of this book, but your exploration of creativity should never end, and I hope it never does.

As we arrive at the final stop of this particular leg of the infinite voyage that is creative discovery, let's pause to make a few final reflections:

What is your biggest insight into creativity that you gained while reading *The World of Creativity*?*

What did you discover about yourself?

How has your World of Creativity expanded, and where are you going next?

Never stop exploring

I will continue to explore creativity. Continue the journey with me on my YouTube channel: @TheCreativityExplorer.

https://www.youtube.com/@TheCreativityExplorer

Bonus chapter

If you are the kind of person who reads every page of a book, including these "extra" pages at the end, you deserve a bonus. I have written one additional chapter, from a 38th country, and

---

*(If you care to share, I would love to know. Email me at fredrik@ fredrikharen.com.)

the only way to get access to that is to email me at fredrik@ fredrikharen.com and write "bonus chapter" as the email headline. It is my way of giving extra value to the really curious reader. ☺

P.S. If I decide to write *The World of Creativity 2*, with more stories, more examples, more insights and lessons into creativity from around the globe, would you be interested in reading it?

If so, email me with the headline 'More' to fredrik@ fredrikharen.com

Reach out and stay in touch

I would love to hear from you.

If you have an interesting story or insight about creativity, do send it to me. And if you know of anyone I should interview about creativity, please introduce us to each other. You can reach me at fredrik@fredrikharen.com.

Newsletter

If you want to get continuous insights into *The World of Creativity*, then I encourage you to sign up for The Creativity Explorer newsletter.

To do that, just send an email to fredrik@fredrikharen.com with the headline 'subscribe', or go to www.FredrikHaren.com and fill out the form.

LinkedIn

At LinkedIn, I regularly share content on creativity.

Follow me there at https://www.linkedin.com/in/fredrikharen, where you can also sign up for The Creativity Explorer LinkedIn newsletter:

https://www.linkedin.com/newsletters/the-creativity-explorer-6967407670718816256/

Speaking

For inquiries for speaking engagements, contact Shehara@ Fredrikharen.com.

Oh, and if you enjoyed exploring creativity with me through this book, then please:

- **Share your insights on your social media and tag me #FredrikHaren or #TheWorldOfCreativity.**

- **Write a review on Amazon or wherever you bought the book.**

It would mean the world to me if you did. It really would.

Thank you

It takes a village to raise a child, and it takes a bunch of people to write a book. My name might be on the cover, but the creative process of making the book happen has been a collaborative process involving hundreds of people.

First of all, of course, I want to thank all the people who are featured in this book. All these wonderful, creative meetings around the world not just made this book happen – they also created lifelong memories for me. I also want to thank all the people who did not make it into this book. I could have written hundreds of additional chapters with insights that came out of the interviews I have conducted, but at some point, you have to draw the line. I hope to share more stories and lessons in future books, posts and videos.

Thank you all!

I also want to take the opportunity to thank: Elaine Haren – for your support and ideas. And for everything.

Thank you:

Lucas Haren
Maria Haren
Sophia Haren

For being patient with me and letting me write. But also, for being such beautiful human beings.

Thank you to all the people who have taken the time to meet with me as I have explored the world of creativity, including all the people featured in this book.

Frank Stephenson
Margit Kunz
Kyoko Yonezawa
Abu Jalal Sarimon
Daan Roosegaarde
Johnson Tsang
Natalia Symeonidou
Yuri Vlasyuk
Iwona Fluda
Saimir Strati
Einar Sandvold
Suzanne Williams
Jo-Dann Darong
Mondo Gascaro
Lukki Viebahn
Chandrika Tamang
Sonam Penjor
Georgina Yen Qin Lee
Ray Mak
Andi Daiszler
Ashley Moran
Lotte Sigh
Hussain Afeef
Dorji Dhradhul
Trang Nguyen
Bam Bi

Manfred Fischer
Axel Klausmeier
Robin Chaurasiya
Ērika Kumerova
Olande Atere
Lars Johannisson
Jorge Vallejo
Derek Sivers
Kevin Cottam
Anna Alsina Bardagí
Amelia
Kevin Lee
Johan Staël von Holstein
Hjalmar Gislason
Auður Ava Ólafsdóttir
Sebastiaan Roestenburg
Sandhya
Mahek
Ayachana
Joy
Kay
Sughra
Batgerel
Binderiya

Others, I would also like to thank:

Berit Härén
Andrew Vine
André Wognum
Anna Bervander
Tish Letticia V. Gilbert

Su Nandar
Lisa Dennis
Michael Scott
Crystal Tan
Pyit Thiri Thaw
Andreas Sigurdsson
Jesper Svenningsen
Lars Sjögren
Jeremy Sturt
Helena Reitberger
Bjørn Ivar Moen
Gustav Gous
Stepan Motejzik
Trevor Ketler
Alexandra Heymowska
Dilay Karatas
Jon Erik Engeset
Gabriella Ekelund
Rajesh Kejriwal
Ola Ahlvarsson
Cornelia Rudh
Ulrika Lundin
Uelkue Schmithuesen
Dainius Baltrušaitis
Niklas Karlsson
Kim Bedwell
Tan Xing Long
Jason Parke
Leon Judovic
Teresa Vencil
Ebba Bonde

Anders Hammarbäck
Patrik Lundholm
Erik Centerlind
Martin Erkhammar
Mats Ahldén
Janicke Eckbo
Mathias Lindholm
Sanna Magnusson
Angelika Holzwarth-Kocher
Göran Olinder
Gustav Palm
Hannah Wennberg
Kuo Pey Juan
Simon Stegrud
Mattias Andersson
Christina Almtun
Reian Werkman
Amy Holt
Christian Ottosson
Morgan Freedude
K Naranbayar
Dilyan Valentinov Peshev
Linsey Nevens
Elaine Holmes
Nandita Kotian
Dennis O Krook
Đorđije Brkuljan
Lorna Scott
Tamar Moise
Jenny Törner
Ange Ortega

Andrej Hanzir
Jacobien Heling
Anders Lagerkvist
Freedom Van Riel
Marijana Borković
Anna Liljehag
Ola Bringle
Patricia Larsen
Darko Buldioski
Luis Eduardo Perez
Lena Nordin-Andersson
Kristian Rovde
Tena Žganec
Kate Bacon
Damian Reid
Dalia Khatibi
Marisol Corominas Manzanedo
Janki Sampat
Karin Lindqvist
Cecilia Cosnard
Agnes Sandström
Monika Kazlauskaite
Anna Uvhagen
Antonio Moz
Anna Fuchs
Muyiwa Fasakin
Michael Schuller
Svetoslava Boyadzhieva
Seun Koshoedo
Kristofer Fröjd
Martins Horta Bernardo

Kristyn Connor
William Yap
Chanel Bornoff
Markus Pizka
Maria Richter
Ville Saarikalle
Chee Li-Fong (Chevaun)
Audrie Fantoni
Mecislavs Maculevics
Anna Bril
Helle Egholm Lorentzen
Laura Garcia
Caroline Cassidy

Jon Brix
Alexander Braun
Jens Boisen
David Sjöland
Selma Ohlsson
Karan Madan
Joanna Walisiak
Lucas P. Gielner
Heather Robinson
Günter Stöffelbauer
Loida Peral
Lucinda Swan
Harrienath Pillay
Mariam Gonzales
Tatjana Marinko
Evelynn Lim
Caroline Hunt

Kenny Gan
Gabriele Winter
Ludivine Costanzo
Joanne Thia
Kate Lossius
Elnaz Fahim
Jonathan Israelson
André Noël Chaker
Susanna Hagelstam
Stefan Cardell
Nina Spegel
Linnea Håkansson
Klaus Carlander
Helena Årstein
Johan Sjöstrand
Susanna Suorsa
Vanja Belacevic
Tanja Barisic-Wirf
Shreya Bhardwaj Pilani
Danish Khan
Pierre Bisaillon
Christine Günther
Cosimo Turroturro
Kelly Macdonald
Priscilla Chan
Tomas Stasiukevičius
Michael Frick
Marianne Holmberg
Florian Schwarz
Knut Meiner

Thank you to the people at Wiley, especially:

Alice Hadaway
Annie Knight
Richard Samson
Deborah Williams

It's been a joy to work with you all, and you made the book so much better.

And finally, thank you to Magnus Lindkvist and Andrew Bryant for being my writing buddies and friends, and to Shehara Alahakoon for organising so many of the interviews and for everything else you do.

Hashtag

Spread the word about *The World of Creativity*. If you want more people to learn from the insights in this book, then **please** share a post on social media and tag the post with #FredrikHaren and #TheWorldOfCreativity.

By doing that, you are making this author extremely happy.

About the Author

Fredrik Haren is *The Creativity Explorer*. He has spent the last 25 years travelling the world to learn as much as he can about human creativity. As *The Creativity Explorer*, he aims to discover more about human creativity, be it from innovators in Silicon Valley or nomads in the desert of Mongolia, to help more people discover their full creative potential. For this work, he has interviewed thousands of creative people all over the world.

Fredrik has been invited to speak more than 2,000 times in more than 75 countries on 6 continents. He is one of the world's most global keynote speakers and speaks in 15-35 countries *per year*. He has been inducted into the 'Speaker Hall of Fame' on two continents, been awarded 'Speaker of The Year' in Sweden and has been selected as one of the 'Top 10 Best Speakers of All Time', also in Sweden.

He is the past president of Asia Professional Speakers Singapore and the founder or co-founder of professional speaker associations in India, Sweden and Bangladesh. He has been awarded 'IAA' by 'The Global Speakers Federation'; one of only 14 professional speakers in the world to receive this designation.

Fredrik has inspired more than one million people from the stage, and over his 25-year professional speaking career, he has been invited to speak by clients in virtually all industries. Clients include Volvo, IKEA, EY, VISA, HP and many, many more.

As *The Creativity Explorer,* he is on a mission to make the world a more creative place.

www.FredrikHaren.com

Fredrik@Fredrikharen.com

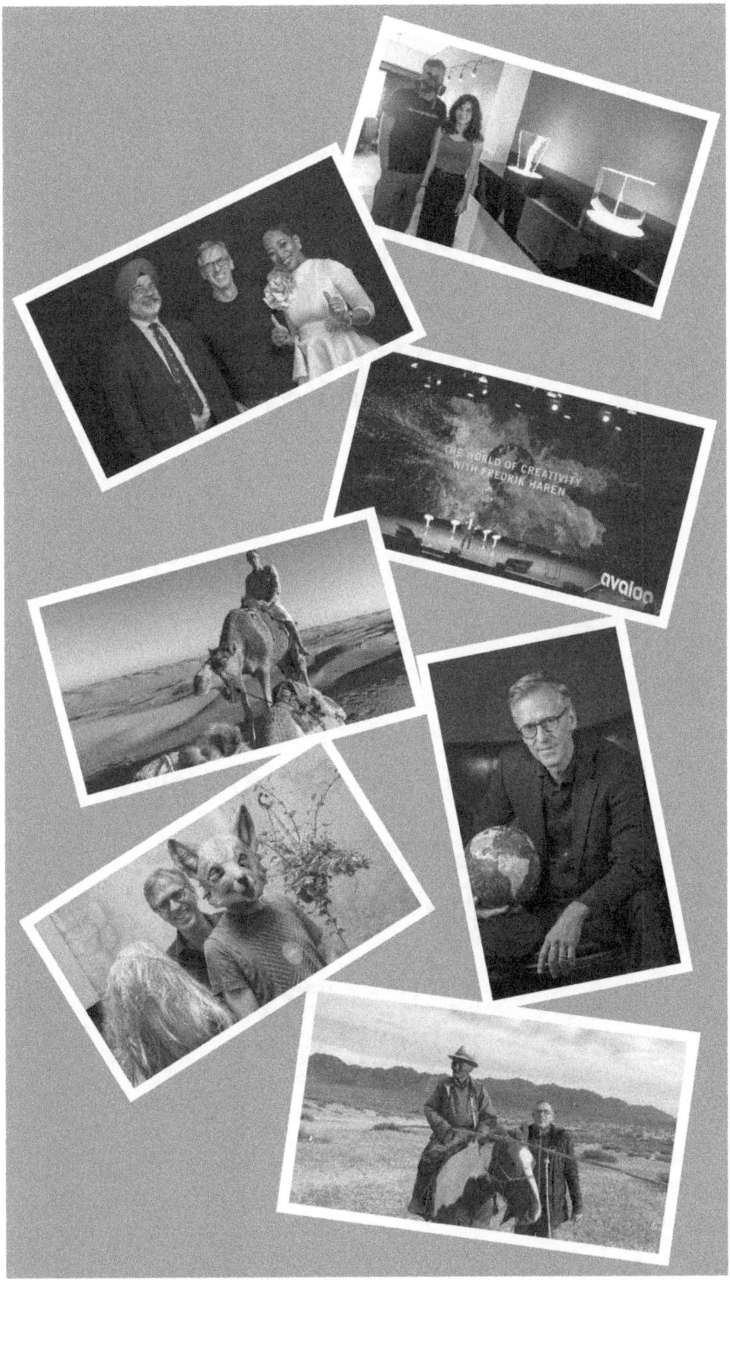
THE WORLD OF CREATIVITY
WITH FREDRIK HAREN
avaloq

Fredrik's LinkedIn profile

YouTube:
Fredrik Haren - The Creativity Explorer

Email: fredrik@fredrikharen.com

The Creativity Explorer Newsletter

https://www.kranti-india.org

Instagram: @johnson_tsang_artist

www.FredrikHaren.com